Wisdom of the
MASTER

Wisdom of the
MASTER

THE SPIRITUAL TEACHINGS OF
'Abdu'l-Bahá

INTRODUCED AND EDITED BY
STEVEN SCHOLL

WHITE CLOUD PRESS
ASHLAND, OREGON
IN ASSOCIATION WITH
KALIMÁT PRESS, LOS ANGELES

97 98 99   5 4 3 2 1

Wisdom of the Master
is published in association with
Kalimat Press, 1600 Sawtelle Blvd., Los Angeles, California 90024.

Cover design by Daniel Cook Design
Printed in Canada

Cloth edition published 1997, ISBN 1-883991-20-X
Paperback edition published 1997, ISBN 1-883991-23-4

LIBRARY OF CONGRESS CATALOGING-IN-PUBLICATION DATA
'Abdu'l-Bahá, 1844-1921.
    [Selections. English. 1997]
    Wisdom of the master : the spiritual teachings of 'Abdu'l-Bahá.
        p. cm.
    Includes bibliographical references (p   ).
    ISBN 1-883991-20-X
    1. 'Abdu'l-Bahá, 1844-1921. I. Title.
BP393.A23   1997
297.9'382--dc21   97-29993
                                                         CIP

Table of Contents

'Abdu'l-Bahá, The Master
in the United States, 1912

Introduction
Steven Scholl

Although not a complete stranger to late twentieth century religious consciousness, 'Abdu'l-Bahá is still a lesser known saint of our age. During his lifetime (1844-1921), he was hailed by the Western press and by leading thinkers as the preeminent representative of liberal religious thought and progressive social action. Much like the Dalai Lama today, 'Abdu'l-Bahá traveled to the West to preach a healing message of religious renewal and universal peace, while also promoting the teachings of his faith. 'Abdu'l-Bahá was thus among what might be designated as the "first wave" of spiritual teachers from the East who ventured to the West to spread the wisdom of their faith traditions.[1]

'Abdu'l-Bahá was known among his followers (the Bahá'ís) and admirers as the Master. Today, the idea of the spiritual master might raise eyebrows. Sadly, we are

too familiar with the sexual scandals, the authoritarian-
ism, and financial corruption of such "religious leaders."
Andrew Harvey's recent books and lectures on the
master/disciple relationship passionately speak of the
dangers of placing one's self under the authority of
another human being.[2] Today we see the beginnings of
a renewal movement in religion that seeks to incorpo-
rate the wisdom of the great spiritual teachers without
the strict controls of a closed relationship between
master and disciple. Popular singer and spiritual
troubador Van Morrison has captured this spirit in the
title of his album: *No Guru, No Method, No Teacher.*

But this spiritual longing for direct connection
with the mystery of the Godhead does not eliminate the
need of the master for those walking the spiritual path.
To try to do away with the master guide is an overreac-
tion to the abusive behavior of some spiritual teachers.
To deny the role of the master is to deny a persistent
and universal spiritual fact: that there are some women
and men who manifest the sacred on earth and communicate it effectively to others. The master can be re-
garded as a permanent and necessary archetype within
human culture. Like other archetypal figures (father,
mother, hero, mentor, trickster) masters can be strong
and true, or they can fall from grace. The existence of
authoritarian or abusive spiritual teachers in our midst

does not negate the positive dimensions of the saint and master any more than the discovery of abusive fathers or mothers requires the end of parenthood.

The master provides a shining proof that there is something more to life than our mundane cares or a purely materialistic philosophy. The master lives in close proximity to the Absolute, to transcendence, and it is this quality of living in mystery and in connection with spiritual power, more than any specific doctrine, that tells us we are in the presence of an authentic spiritual guide. From my reading and experience, there are other signs that help us distinguish a true master from the ego-driven teacher.

First, the true master always remembers that he or she is, like the rest of us, susceptible to ego. 'Abdu'l-Bahá, for example, constantly prayed to God for guidance, wisdom, and humility. He knew that in each moment he was experiencing the Absolute, and yet, paradoxically, in each moment he remained infinitely distant from God, susceptible to the temptations of the lower self, just like every man and woman on earth.

Second, a true master seeks nothing, for he has found true power in the Absolute. In fact, by seeking nothing (or, one might say, seeking emptiness) the master paradoxically uncovers a wealth of spiritual riches. Thus, the master is not driven by the trappings of worldly power or the need to be a leader. He is led by the spirit, and he leads others by the power of his example.

Third, in the life of a master, there is a magical blending of depth and simplicity, so that each action is an act of grace, every teaching emerges from direct experience of the Holy, and every effort is toward bringing joy and healing to those who are touched by sorrow and suffering.

In brief, the master's life is a life of service; his life becomes a prayer and his prayers "transcend the murmur of syllables and sounds," becoming pure spirit that illumines the hearts of those who enter his or her presence.

'Abdu'l-Bahá, though no longer with us physically, remains an example of a true master. His life and teachings continue to speak to our needs and concerns as we approach the new millennium. Indeed, the power of his deeds and the clarity of his beliefs are more relevant than ever in this time of transition and crisis. As the divide between rich and poor grows, as the slaughters brought on by ethnic and religious conflicts spread, 'Abdu'l-Bahá's powerful message of unity and reconciliaiton becomes even more important to our world.

'Abdu'l-Bahá's teachings grew out of those of his father, Bahá'u'lláh (1817-1892), a messianic figure who claimed to be the long-awaited world teacher that many religious traditions speak of appearing "at the end of time." Bahá'u'lláh brought a message of religious tolerance, seeking to find points of harmony between religions, calling for an end to all forms of religious exclusivism and prejudice. Saying that humanity had reached a new level of collective wisdom and maturity, Bahá'u'lláh sought to create a religious community that was egalitarian, democratic, and characterized by racial and sexual equality. He encouraged the independent investigation of truth, spoke of the need for religion and science to balance each other's truth claims, and called for the creation of international agencies for disarmament and collective security.

Interestingly, he eliminated the priestly class from his communal experiment in truth, saying it was religious leaders who most often created serious conflict in the world by their strict adherence to literal interpretations of their sacred scripture. In books and prayers, Bahá'u'lláh offered a profound and deeply mystical teaching that revolves around the metaphysical principle of unity and multiplicity within the Godhead in its transcendent and immanent dimensions. In short, the ethical and spiritual teachings of Bahá'u'lláh and his son are centered on the principle of unity in diversity.

Bahá'u'lláh and his followers fearlessly proclaimed

these teachings within the heart of a conservative
Islamic culture in the later part of the last century.
Not surprisingly, his views were not welcomed by the
powers of his time. Bahá'u'lláh was imprisoned in 1852,
and spent the rest of his life a prisoner and in exile for
his reform efforts.[3]

'Abdu'l-Bahá was eight years old when his father
was imprisoned. He joined Bahá'u'lláh in exile, and was
only released from captivity in 1908, at the age of 64.
Considered "a dangerous man" by the political and
religious leaders of his time, he quietly went about his
business, feeding the poor, providing spiritual guidance
to all who sought him out, and working tirelessly for
peace and reconciliation throughout the world. His
captors soon came to respect him and many of his
enemies became his devoted and trusted friends. (See
pages 9-10 of this book for an example of one man who
went from hatred to love due to the persistent care
showered upon him by 'Abdu'l-Bahá.)

As soon as he was released from captivity, 'Abdu'l-
Bahá began his world travels to spread the cause of
racial unity and world peace. He was hailed as the
"prophet of peace," a man who "walked the mystical
path with pratical feet." As you will find in the stories
that follow, his life was truly that of the spiritual master.
He lived in the moment and always found a way to shed

light in the darkness—whether by giving away the
pants he was wearing to a homeless seeker or demand-
ing that the gathering he attended be integrated, even if
it violated the racial segregation laws of Washington,
D.C., in 1912.

In 1921, his life of service to humanity and surren-
der to God came to an end. The outpouring of grief and
affection that followed was unprecedented in the
history of Palestine, 'Abdu'l-Bahá's home-in-exile. His
funeral procession in Haifa brought together Jew and
Christian, Muslim and Druze, Armenians and Turks,
Persians and Arabs, Europeans and Americans. This
remarkable gathering of disparate and often conflicting
communities was symbolic of the unity in diversity that
'Abdu'l-Bahá sought throughout his long life of service.

With this book, I have attempted to bring together
a representative selection of 'Abdu'l-Bahá's writings on
the religious life and a few descriptions of his life and
the power of his presence written by those who encoun-
tered his gentle majesty. This is a long overdue introduction for Western audiences of the man so many
loved, admired, and called the Master.

FOOTNOTES

1. Other first wave spiritual teachers include Swami
Vivekananda (Vedanta/Ramakrishna Mission), Hazrat Inayat
Khan (Sufism) Paramahansa Yogananda (Self Realization
Fellowship), and D. T. Suzuki (Zen Buddhism).

2. Andrew Harvey, *The Return of the Mother* (Berkeley:
Frog Ltd., 1996). Harvey sees this longing by the spiritual
seeker to submit to the master as an infantile wish to return
to the safety of a parental relationship that may have been
underdeveloped or tragically distorted. Also see Rita Gross,
"Guru, God, and Gender: Issues in the Modern Teacher/
Student Relationship" *Shambhala Sun* (July 1997) on recent
allegations of sexual misconduct by Tibetan Buddhist
spiritual teachers.

3. Not all of his life was spent in jails. He was many
times under house arrest, or simply confined to a city,
though there were several occasions when the imprisonment
was harsh and his life and those of his followers were in
jeopardy. See Juan Cole, *Modernity and the Millennium: The
Genesis of the Baha'i Faith in the Nineteenth-Century Middle East*
(New York: Columbia University Press, 1998) for the best
academic introduction to the life and teachings of
Bahá'u'lláh. See also, H. M. Balyuzi, *Baha'u'llah: The King of
Glory* (Oxford: George Ronald, 1980) and Shoghi Effendi,
God Passes By (Wilmette, Ill.: Bahá'í Publishing Trust, 1944).

Portrait of 'Abdu'l-Bahá
by Juliet Thompson, 1912

1

The Master

Servant of Humanity

S eldom have I seen one whose appearance
impressed me more. A tall strongly-built man
holding himself straight as an arrow, with white
turban and raiment, long black locks reaching almost to
the shoulder, broad powerful forehead indicating a
strong intellect combined with an unswerving will, eyes
keen as a hawk's, and strongly-marked but pleasing
features—such was my first impression of 'Abbás Efendí,
'the master' (Áqá) as he *par excellence* is called by the
Bábís. Subsequent conversation with him served only to
heighten the respect with which his appearance had

from the first inspired me. One more eloquent of
speech, more ready of argument, more apt of illustra-
tion, more intimately acquainted with the sacred books
of the Jews, the Christians, and the Muhammadans,
could, I should think, scarcely be found even amongst
the eloquent, ready, and subtle race to which he be-
longs. These qualities, combined with a bearing at once
majestic and genial, made me cease to wonder at the
influence and esteem which he enjoyed even beyond
the circle of his father's followers. About the greatness
of this man and his power no one who had seen him
could entertain a doubt.[1]

Imagine that we are in the ancient house of the still
more ancient city of 'Akká, which was for a month my
home. The room in which we are faces the opposite
wall of a narrow paved street, which an active man
might clear at a single bound. Above is the bright sun of
Palestine; to the right a glimpse of the old sea-wall and
the blue Mediterranean. As we sit we hear a singular
sound rising from the pavement, thirty feet below—
faint at first, and increasing. It is like the murmur of
human voices. We open the window and look down.
We see a crowd of human beings with patched and

tattered garments. Let us descend to the street and see who these are.

It is a noteworthy gathering. Many of these men are blind; many more are pale, emaciated, or aged. Some are on crutches; some are so feeble that they can barely walk. Most of the women are closely veiled, but enough are uncovered to cause us well to believe that, if the veils were lifted, more pain and misery would be seen. Some of them carry babes with pinched and sallow faces. There are perhaps a hundred in this gathering, and besides, many children. They are of all the races one meets in these streets—Syrians, Arabs, Ethiopians, and many others.

These people are ranged against the walls or seated on the ground, apparently in an attitude of expectation;—for what do they wait? Let us wait with them.

We have not to wait long. A door opens and a man comes out. He is of middle stature, strongly built. He wears flowing light-colored robes. On his head is a light buff fez with a white cloth wound about it. He is perhaps sixty years of age. His long grey hair rests on his shoulders. His forehead is broad, full, and high, his nose slightly aquiline, his moustaches and beard, the latter full though not heavy, nearly white. His eyes are grey and blue, large, and both soft and penetrating. His bearing is simple, but there is grace, dignity, and even majesty about his movements. He passes through the crowd, and as he goes utters words of salutation. We do not understand them, but we see the benignity and the kindliness of his countenance. He stations himself at a narrow angle of the street and motions to the people to come towards him. They crowd up a little too insistently. He pushes them gently back and lets them pass him one by one. As they come they hold their hands extended. In each open palm he places some small coins. He knows them all. He caresses them with his hand on the face, on the shoulders, on the head. Some he stops and questions. An aged Negro who hobbles up, he greets with some kindly inquiry; the old man's broad face breaks into a sunny smile, his white teeth glistening against his ebony skin as he replies. He stops a woman with a babe and fondly strokes the child. As they pass, some kiss his hand. To all he says, *"Marhabá, marhabá"*— "Well done, well done!"

So they all pass him. The children have been crowding around him with extended hands, but to them he has not given. However, at the end, as he turns to go, he throws a handful of coppers over his shoulders, for which they scramble.

During this time this friend of the poor has not been unattended. Several men wearing red fezes, and with earnest and kindly faces, followed him from the

The Master at Home
in Palestine with a child.

house, stood near him and aided in regulating the
crowd, and now, with reverent manner and at a respect-
ful distance, follow him away. When they address him
they call him "Master." This scene you may see almost
any day of the year in the streets of 'Akká.[2]

In the cold weather which is approaching, the poor will
suffer, for, as in all cities, they are thinly clad. Some day
at this season, if you are advised of the place and time,
you may see the poor of 'Akká gathered at one of the
shops where clothes are sold, receiving cloaks from the
Master. Upon many, especially the most infirm or
crippled, he himself places the garment, adjusts it with
his own hands, and strokes it approvingly, as if to say,
"There! Now you will do well." There are five or six
hundred poor in 'Akká, to all of whom he gives a warm
garment each year.

On feast days he visit the poor at their homes. He
chats with them, inquires into their health and comfort,
mentions by name those who are absent, and leaves
gifts for all.

Nor is it the beggars only that he remembers.
Those respectable poor who cannot beg, but must suffer
in silence—those whose daily labor will not support
their families—to these he sends bread secretly. His left

hand knoweth not what his right hand doeth.

All the people know him and love him—the rich and the poor, the young and the old—even the babe leaping in its mother's arms. If he hears of any one sick in the city—Muslim or Christian, or of any other sect, it matters not—he is each day at their bedside, or sends a trusty messenger. If a physician is needed, and the patient poor, he brings or sends one, and also the necessary medicine. If he finds a leaking roof or a broken window menacing health, he summons a work-man, and waits himself to see the breach repaired. If any one is in trouble,—if a son or a brother is thrown into prison, or he is threatened at law, or falls into any difficulty too heavy for him—it is to the Master that he straightway makes appeal for counsel or for aid. Indeed, for counsel all come to him, rich as well as poor. He is the kind father of all the people.[3]

The Master at Work

During the winter of 1919-1920 the writer had the great privilege of spending two and a half months as the guest of 'Abdu'l-Bahá at Haifa and intimately observing His daily life. At that time, although nearly seventy-six years of age, He was still remarkably vigorous, and accom-plished daily an almost incredible amount of work.

'Abdu'l-Bahá

Although often very weary He showed wonderful powers of recuperation, and His services were always at the disposal of those who needed them most. His unfailing patience, gentleness, kindliness, and tact made His presence like a benediction.

It was His custom to spend a large part of each night in prayer and meditation. From early morning until evening, except for a short siesta after lunch, He was busily engaged in reading and answering letters from many lands and in attending to the multitudinous affairs of the household and of the Cause. In the afternoon He usually had a little relaxation in the form of a walk or a drive, but even then He was usually accompanied by one or two, or a party, of pilgrims with whom He would converse on spiritual matters, or He would find opportunity by the way of seeing and ministering to some of the poor. After His return He would call the friends to the usually evening meeting in His salon. Both at lunch and supper He used to entertain a number of pilgrims and friends, and charm His guests with happy and humorous stories as well as precious talks on a great variety of subjects. "My home is the home of laughter and mirth," He declared, and indeed it was so. He delighted in gathering together people of various races, colors, nations, and religions in unity and cordial friendship around His hospitable board. He was indeed a loving father not only to the little community at Haifa, but to the Bahá'í community throughout the world.[4]

For more than thirty-four years this man has been a prisoner at 'Akká. But his jailors have become his friends. The governor of the city, the commander of the Army Corps, respect and honor him as though he were their brother. No man's opinion or recommendation has greater weight with them. He is the beloved of all the city, high and low. And how could it be otherwise? For to this man it is the law, as it was to Jesus of Nazareth, to do good to those who injure him. Have we yet heard of any one in lands which boast the name of Christ who lived that life?

Hear how he treats his enemies. One instance of many I have heard will suffice.

When the Master came to 'Akká there lived there a certain man from Afghanistan, an austere and rigid Mussulman. To him the Master was a heretic. He felt and nourished a great enmity towards the Master, and roused up others against him. When opportunity offered in gatherings of the people, as in the Mosque, he denounced him with bitter words.

"This man," he said to all, "is an imposter. Why do you speak to him? Why do you have dealings with him?" And when he passed the Master on the street he was careful to hold his robe before his face that his sight might not be defiled.

Thus did this Afghan. The Master, however, did thus: The Afghan was poor and lived in a mosque; he was frequently in need of food and clothing. The Master sent him both. These he accepted, but without thanks. He fell sick. The Master took him a physician, food, medicine, money. These, also, he accepted; but as he held out one hand that the physician might take his pulse, with the other he held his cloak before his face that he might not look upon the Master. For twenty-four years the Master continued his kindnesses and the Afghan persisted in his enmity. Then at last one day the Afghan came to the Master's door, and fell down, penitent and weeping, at his feet.

"Forgive me, sir!" he cried. "For twenty-four years I have done evil to you, for twenty-four years you have done good to me. Now I know that I have been in the wrong."

The Master bade him rise and they became friends.

This Master is as simple as his soul is great. He claims nothing for himself—neither comfort, nor honor, nor repose. Three or four hours of sleep suffice him; all the remainder of his time and all his strength are given to the succor of those who suffer, in spirit or in body. "I am," he says, "the servant of God."[5]

The Master in the West

If I could only picture to you Abdul-Baha in the West; Abdul-Baha with the power of his peace in the restless West; Abdul-Baha in the complex West with the power of his simplicity; Abdul-Baha with his noble and illumined beauty in the artificial and skeptical West;—so strongly defined in his completeness against our undevelopment![6]

When the ship [arriving in New York harbor] was abreast the Statue of Liberty, standing erect and facing it, Abdul-Baha held his arms wide apart in salutation, and said:

"There is the new world's symbol of liberty and freedom. After being forty years a prisoner I can tell you that freedom is not a matter of place. It is a condition. Unless one accept dire vicissitudes he will not attain. When one is released from the prison of self, that is indeed a release."

Then, waving adieu to the Statue of Liberty, he continued:

"In former ages it has been said, 'To love one's native land is faith.' But the tongue in this day says. 'Glory is not his who loves his native land; but glory is his who loves his kind—humanity.'"

"What is your attitude toward woman suffrage?" asked one of the reporters.

"The modern suffragette is fighting for what must be, and many of these are willing martyrs to imprisonment for their cause. . . .

"The world in the past has been ruled by force, and man has dominated over woman by reason of his more forceful and aggressive qualities both of body and mind. But the scales are already shifting—force is losing its weight and mental alertness, intuition, and the spiritual qualities of love and service, in which woman is strong, are gaining ascendancy. Hence the new age will be an age less masculine, and more permeated with the feminine ideals—or, to speak more exactly, will be an age in which the masculine and feminine elements of civilization will be more properly balanced."

"What is a Bahai?" asked one of the reporters.

"To be a Bahai simply means to love all the world, to love humanity and try to serve it; to work for Universal Peace, and Universal Brotherhood," replied Abdul-Baha.

The ship now pointed its nose up the North River,

and, gazing in a look of bewildered amazement at the
rugged skyline of the lower city formed by the down-
town skyscrapers, the "Wise Man out of the East,"
remarked, pointing at towering buildings:

"These are the minarets of Western World com-
merce and industry, and seem to stretch these things
heavenward in an endeavor to bring about this Universal Peace for which we are all working, for the good of
the nations and mankind in general."[7]

Friends have asked me to describe 'Abdu'l-Bahá. How
can anyone describe Him? Each one of us saw Him with
our own spiritual and physical eyes. It seemed that in
Him we found what we most longed for. In the Master's
presence I felt as though I were in another world. In
those moments I seemed most conscious of His over-
powering love for all mankind. From childhood 'Abdu'l-
Bahá had been endowed with physical beauty, we are
told. Despite His advanced age and the vicissitudes He
had endured, His carriage was majestic and His posture
remarkable. He seemed to me to be about five feet, nine
inches tall, although His long 'abá and His white turban
may have caused Him to appear taller than He was. He
was strong and vibrant. He walked lightly, so that there

'Abdu'l-Bahá in Oakland, California, 1912

were moments when He seemed hardly to touch the ground.

'Abdu'l-Bahá enjoyed walking. His secretaries usually accompanied Him. On the street people would turn and glance at Him, and many curious eyes followed Him as He strolled along with great dignity and grace in His Eastern robe and turban. 'Abdu'l-Bahá always wore His native dress, which was a full-length, light-colored robe, over which He wore an 'abá, or cloak, of beige, tan, brown, or cream color. His shoes were of soft brown leather, partly covering the instep and heel. He wore a low turban wound around with folds of soft

14

white material from under which His wispy silver hair fell to His shoulders. Encircling His often-smiling lips was a white mustache and a short, rounded beard. The Master had well-defined, slightly bushy, white eyebrows. To the astonishment of each person who talked with Him, His eyes seemed to change color as He spoke. Sometimes they looked blue or hazel or grey, with a tiny white line encircling the iris. . . .

When the Master's face was in repose, deep lines often appeared on His cheeks and between His brows, and His eyes looked sad and showed the suffering He had endured. However, when 'Abdu'l-Bahá smiled, the sadness vanished, and one saw only glorious beauty in His face, especially when He spoke of His Father's principles. The Master's complexion was a warm, light tan. His hands were square, strong, yet delicate; when He held your hand, His clasp felt warm and friendly.

As with His eyes so did 'Abdu'l-Bahá's voice change when He spoke on different subjects. At times it was soft and gentle, low and penetrating; or it was loud and firm. His language was always exquisite. His pleasing, musical tones touched our hearts as He chanted a prayer. Despite the Master's fatigue at times, and His physical ailments, He welcomed everyone with a beaming smile, and in His pleasing and vibrant voice would ask, "Are you happy?"

He loved the sound of laughter and often told stories and anecdotes to make us laugh. When we heard Him laugh, we knew that He or someone else had told an amusing story, and the sound of His laughter made us all happy.[8]

When he reached the Occident . . . Abdul-Baha faced a condition which troubled him greatly, because it was beyond his power to assuage the misery he saw constantly about him. Housed luxuriously at Cadogan Gardens, London, he knew that within a stone's throw of him were people who had never had enough to eat—and in New York there was exactly the same situation. These things made him exceedingly sad, and he said: "The time will come in the near future when humanity will become so much more sensitive than at present that the man of great wealth will not enjoy his luxury, in comparison with the deplorable poverty about him. He will be forced, for his own happiness, to expend his wealth to procure better conditions for the community in which he lives."

When Abdul-Baha first arrived in England he was the guest of a friend in a village not far from London. The evident poverty around him in this wealthy coun-

'Abdu'l-Bahá in America

try distressed him greatly. He would walk out in the
town, garbed in his white turban and long Persian coat,
and all eyes were centered upon this strange visitor,
who, the people had been told, was "a holy man from
the East." Naturally the children were attracted to him,
followed him, pulled at his coat, or his hand, and were
immediately taken into his arms and caressed. This
delighted them, of course, and children are never afraid
of Abdul-Baha, but what pleased and amazed them still
more was that when they were put down they found in
their little hands a shilling or sixpence from the capa-
cious pockets of "the holy man's" long coat. Such bits of
silver were a rarity in their experience, and they ran
home with joy to tell the tale of the generous stranger
from the Orient, possessed apparently of an endless
store of shining sixpences.

The children crowded after him and so many
sixpences were dispensed that the friend who enter-
tained Abdul-Baha became alarmed, and talked the
matter over with Miss Robarts, who was also a guest in
the house. "It is a shame!" they said indignantly. "He
comes to us accepting nothing, and is giving to our
people all the time! It must not go on!"

That day Abdul-Baha had bestowed many sixpences, and people had come from the neighboring
villages, bringing their children to receive the blessing

from "the holy man,"—and of course the sixpences! About nine o'clock in the evening the ladies decided that no one else must see Abdul-Baha that night. But as they waited outside the cottage, a man came up the path, carrying one baby, and with others clinging to him. When he asked for "the holy man," however, he was told severely that he could not be seen, he was very tired and had gone to bed. The man sighed, as he said, "Oh, I have walked six miles from far away to see him. I am so sorry!"

The hostess responded severely, feeling that the desire for sixpences had prompted the journey perhaps more than religious enthusiasm, and the man sighed more deeply than ever, and was turning away, when suddenly Abdul-Baha came around the corner of the house. The way in which he embraced the man and all the babies was so wonderful, that the hearts of the too careful friends melted within them, and when he at last sent away the unbidden guests, comforted, their hearts full of joy, their hands bursting with sixpences, the two friends looked at one another and said: "How wrong we were! We will never again try to manage Abdul-Baha!"[9]

'Abdu'l-Bahá as a young man of twenty-four
in Ottoman Turkey

II

Personal Transformation

Journey of the Soul

K now that nothing which exists remains in a state of repose—that is to say, all things are in motion. Everything is either growing or declining; all things are either coming from nonexistence into being, or going from existence into nonexistence. So this flower, this hyacinth, during a certain period of time was coming from the world of nonexistence into being, and now it is going from being into nonexistence. This state of motion is said to be essential—that is, natural; it cannot be separated from beings because it is their essential requirement, as it is the essential requirement of fire to burn.[10]

Now let us consider the soul. We have seen that movement is essential to existence; nothing that has life is without motion. All creation, whether of the mineral, vegetable or animal kingdom, is compelled to obey the law of motion; it must either ascend or descend. But with the human soul, there is no decline. Its only movement is towards perfection; growth and progress alone constitute the motion of the soul.

Divine perfection is infinite, therefore the progress of the soul is also infinite. From the very birth of a human being the soul progresses, the intellect grows and knowledge increases. When the body dies the soul lives on. All the differing degrees of created physical beings are limited, but the soul is limitless! . . .

In the world of spirit there is no retrogression. The world of mortality is a world of contradictions, of opposites; motion being compulsory everything must either go forward or retreat. In the realm of spirit there is no retreat possible, all movement is bound to be towards a perfect state. 'Progress' is the expression of spirit in the world of matter. The intelligence of man,

22

his reasoning powers, his knowledge, his scientific achievements, all these being manifestations of the spirit, partake of the inevitable law of spiritual progress and are, therefore, of necessity, immortal.

My hope for you is that you will progress in the world of spirit, as well as in the world of matter; that your intelligence will develop, your knowledge will augment, and your understanding be widened.

You must ever press forward, never standing still; avoid stagnation, the first step to a backward movement, to decay.[11]

We must not be content with simply following a certain course because we find our fathers pursued that course. . . . Every man must be an investigator for himself. Ideas and beliefs left by his fathers and ancestors as a heritage will not suffice, for adherence to these are but imitations, and imitations have ever been a cause of disappointment and misguidance. Be investigators of reality that you may attain the verity of truth and life.[12]

God has given man the eye of investigation by which he may see and recognize truth. He has endowed man with ears that he may hear the message of reality and conferred upon him the gift of reason by which he may discover things for himself. This is his endowment and equipment for the investigation of reality.

Man is not intended to see through the eyes of another, hear through another's ears nor comprehend with another's mind. Each human creature has individual endowment, power and responsibility in the creative plan of God.

Therefore, depend upon your own reason and judgment and adhere to the outcome of your own investigation; otherwise, you will be utterly submerged in the sea of ignorance and deprived of all the bounties of God.

Turn to God, supplicate humbly at His threshold, seeking assistance and confirmation, that God may rend asunder the veils that obscure your vision. Then will your eyes be filled with illumination, face to face you will behold the reality of God and your heart become completely purified from the dross of ignorance, reflecting the glories and bounties of the Kingdom.

Holy souls are like soil which has been plowed and tilled with much earnest labor, the thorns and thistles cast aside and all weeds uprooted. Such soil is most fruitful, and the harvest from it will prove full and plenteous. In this same way man must free himself from the weeds of ignorance, thorns of superstitions and thistles of imitations that he may discover reality in the harvest of true knowledge. . . .

Just now the soil of human hearts seems like black earth, but in the innermost substance of this dark soil there are thousands of fragrant flowers latent. We must endeavor to cultivate and awaken these potentialities, discover the secret treasure in this very mine and depository of God, bring forth these resplendent powers long hidden in human hearts. Then will the glories of both worlds be blended and increased and the quintessence of human existence be made manifest. . . .

It is evident, therefore, that man is in need of divine education and inspiration, that the spirit and bounties of God are essential to his development. That is to say, the teachings of Christ and the Prophets are necessary for his education and guidance. Why? Because They are the divine Gardeners Who till the earth of human hearts and minds. They educate man, uproot the weeds, burn the thorns and remodel the waste places into gardens and orchards where fruitful trees grow. The wisdom and purpose of Their training is that man must pass from degree to degree of progressive unfoldment until perfection is attained. For instance, if a man should live his entire life in one city, he cannot gain a knowledge of the whole world. To become perfectly informed he must visit other cities, see the mountains and valleys, cross the rivers and traverse the plains. In other words, without progressive and universal education perfection will not be attained.

Man must walk in many paths and be subjected to various processes in his evolution upward. Physically he is not born in full stature but passes through consecutive stages of fetus, infant, childhood, youth, maturity and old age. Suppose he had the power to remain young throughout his life. He then would not understand the meaning of old age and could not believe it existed. If he could not realize the condition of age, he would not know that he was young. He would not know the difference between young and old without experiencing the old. Unless you have passed through the state of infancy, how would you know this was an infant beside you? . . .

Briefly, the journey of the soul is necessary. The pathway of life is the road which leads to divine knowledge and attainment. Without training and guidance the soul could never progress beyond the conditions of its lower nature.[13]

'Abdu'l-Bahá in Haifa, Palestine

Love: The Foundation of Faith

We declare that love is the cause the existence of all phenomena and that the absence of love is the cause of disintegration or nonexistence. Love is the conscious bestowal of God, the bond of affiliation in all phenomena.[14]

Love is the cause of God's revelation unto man, the vital bond inherent, in accordance with the divine creation, in the realities of things.[15]

The first sign of faith is love. The message of the holy, divine Manifestations is love; the phenomena of creation are based on love; the radiance of the world is due to love; the well-being and happiness of the world depend on it.[16]

Love is the source of all the bestowals of God. Until love takes possession of the heart, no other divine bounty can be revealed in it.[17]

Know thou of a certainty that Love is the secret of
God's holy Dispensation, the manifestation of the All-
Merciful, the fountain of spiritual outpourings. Love is
heaven's kindly light, the Holy Spirit's eternal breath
that vivifieth the human soul. Love is the cause of God's
revelation unto man, the vital bond inherent, in accordance with the divine creation, in the realities of things.
Love is the one means that ensureth true felicity both in
this world and the next. Love is the light that guideth in
darkness, the living link that uniteth God with man,
that assureth the progress of every illumined soul. Love
is the most great law that ruleth this mighty and heavenly cycle, the unique power that bindeth together the
divers elements of this material world, the supreme
magnetic force that directeth the movements of the
spheres in the celestial realms. Love revealeth with
unfailing and limitless power the mysteries latent in the
universe. Love is the spirit of life unto the adorned body
of mankind, the establisher of true civilization in this
mortal world, and the shedder of imperishable glory
upon every high-aiming race and nation. . . .

O ye beloved of the Lord! Strive to become the
manifestations of the love of God, the lamps of divine
guidance shining amongst the kindreds of the earth
with the light of love and concord.

All hail to the revealers of this glorious light![18]

Love is the real magnet which attracts the hearts and souls of men, and consequently the purpose of the manifestations of God is to radiate the light of love from their hearts. That is why Jesus said, "I am Love." Thus it becomes known that the highest human station, the chief virtue, the cause of the greatest progress and prosperity which humanity can attain, and the divine perfection of the human race is love, which is the greatest favor of the Majestic One. This is the Divine Light, the eternal life. All the Divine Manifestations and prophets taught this truth, and the purpose of all of them was love.[19]

Love is greater than peace, for peace is founded upon love. Love is the objective point of peace, and peace is an outcome of love. Until love is attained, peace cannot be. . . . The love which is from God is the fundamental. This love is the object of all human attainment, the radiance of heaven, the light of man.[20]

Love gives life to the lifeless. Love lights a flame in the

heart that is cold. Love brings hope to the hopeless and gladdens the hearts of the sorrowful. In the world of existence there is indeed no greater power than the power of love.[21]

If I love you, I need not continually speak of my love—you will know without any words.[22]

True Wealth

O ye loved ones of God!

Know ye that the world is even as a mirage rising over the sands, that the thirsty mistaketh for water. The wine of this world is but a vapor in the desert, its pity and compassion but toil and trouble, the repose it proffereth only weariness and sorrow. Abandon it to those who belong to it, and turn your faces unto the Kingdom of your Lord the All-Merciful, that His grace and bounty may cast their dawning splendors over you, and a heavenly table may be sent down for you, and your Lord may bless you, and shower His riches upon you to gladden your bosoms and fill your hearts with bliss, to attract your minds, and cleanse your souls, and console your eyes.[23]

31

❀

The honor and exaltation of man must be something
more than material riches. Material comforts are only a
branch, but the root of the exaltation of man is the
good attributes and virtues which are the adornments of
his reality. These are the divine appearances, the heavenly bounties, the sublime emotions, the love and
knowledge of God; universal wisdom, intellectual
perception, scientific discoveries, justice, equity, truthfulness, benevolence, natural courage and innate forti-
tude; the respect for rights and the keeping of agree-
ments and covenants; rectitude in all circumstances;
serving the truth under all conditions; the sacrifice of
one's life for the good of all people; kindness and esteem
for all nations; obedience to the teachings of God;
service in the Divine Kingdom; the guidance of the
people, and the education of the nations and races. This
is the prosperity of the human world! This is the exaltation of man in the world! This is eternal life and heavenly honor!

These virtues do not appear from the reality of
man except through the power of God and the divine
teachings, for they need supernatural power for their
manifestation. It may be that in the world of nature a
trace of these perfections may appear, but they are

unstable and ephemeral; they are like the rays of the sun upon the wall.

As the compassionate God has placed such a wonderful crown upon the head of man, man should strive that its brilliant jewels may become visible in the world.[24]

These few brief days shall pass away, this present life shall vanish from our sight; the roses of this world shall be fresh and fair no more, the garden of this earth's triumphs and delights shall droop and fade. The spring season of life shall turn into the autumn of death, the bright joy of palace halls give way to moonless dark within the tomb. And therefore is none of this worth loving at all, and to this the wise will not anchor his heart.

He who hath knowledge and power will rather seek out the glory of heaven, and spiritual distinction, and the life that dieth not. And such a one longeth to approach the sacred Threshold of God; for in the tavern of this swiftly-passing world the man of God will not lie drunken, nor will he even for a moment take his ease, nor stain himself with any fondness for this earthly life.[25]

'Abdu'l-Bahá

Soon will your swiftly-passing days be over, and the fame and riches, the comforts, the joys provided by this rubbish-heap, the world, will be gone without a trace. Summon ye, then, the people to God, and invite humanity to follow the example of the Company on high. Be ye loving fathers to the orphan, and a refuge to the helpless, and a treasury for the poor, and a cure for the ailing. Be ye the helpers of every victim of oppression, the patrons of the disadvantaged. Think ye at all times of rendering some service to every member of the human race. Pay ye no heed to aversion and rejection, to disdain, hostility, injustice: act ye in the opposite way.

Be ye sincerely kind, not in appearance only. Let each one of God's loved ones center his attention on this: to be the Lord's mercy to man; to be the Lord's grace. Let him do some good to every person whose path he crosseth, and be of some benefit to him. Let him improve the character of each and all, and reorient the minds of men. In this way, the light of divine guidance will shine forth, and the blessings of God will cradle all mankind: for love is light, no matter in what abode it dwelleth; and hate is darkness, no matter where it may make its nest.

'Abdu'l-Bahá, the Master

O friends of God! That the hidden Mystery may stand revealed, and the secret essence of all things may be disclosed, strive ye to banish that darkness for ever and ever.[26]

Reflections in a Mirror

The mission of the Prophets, the revelation of the Holy Books, the manifestation of the heavenly Teachers and the purpose of divine philosophy all center in the training of the human realities so that they may become clear and pure as mirrors and reflect the light and love of the Sun of Reality. Therefore, I hope that—whether you be in the East or the West—you will strive with heart and soul in order that day by day the world of humanity may become glorified, more spiritual, more sanctified; and that the splendor of the Sun of Reality may be revealed fully in human hearts as in a mirror. This is worthy of the world of mankind. This is the true evolution and progress of humanity. This is the supreme bestowal.

Otherwise, by simple development along material lines man is not perfected. At most, the physical aspect of man, his natural or material conditions, may become stabilized and improved, but he will remain deprived of the spiritual or divine bestowal. He is then like a body

36

without a spirit, a lamp without the light, an eye without the power of vision, an ear that hears no sound, a mind incapable of perceiving, an intellect minus the power of reason.[27]

The Divine Reality is Unthinkable, Limitless, Eternal, Immortal and Invisible.

The world of creation is bound by natural law, finite and mortal.

The Infinite Reality cannot be said to ascend or descend. It is beyond the understanding of man, and cannot be described in terms which apply to the phenomenal sphere of the created world.

Man, then, is in extreme need of the only Power by which he is able to receive help from the Divine Reality, that Power alone bringing him into contact with the Source of all life.

An intermediary is needed to bring two extremes into relation with each other. Riches and poverty, plenty and need: without an intermediary power there could be no relation between the pairs of opposites.

So we can say there must a Mediator between God and Man, and this is none other than the Holy Spirit, which brings the created earth into relation with the 'Unthinkable One,' the Divine Reality.

The Divine Reality may be likened to the sun and the Holy Spirit to the rays of the sun. As the rays of the sun bring the light and warmth of the sun to the earth, giving life to all created beings, so do the Manifestations [i.e., great founders of the world's religions] bring the power of the Holy Spirit from the Divine Sun of Reality to give light and life to the souls of man.

Behold, there is an intermediary necessary between the sun and the earth; the sun does not descend to the earth, neither does the earth ascend to the sun. This contact is made by the rays of the sun which bring light and warmth and heat.

The Holy Spirit is the Light from the Sun of Truth bringing, by its infinite power, life and illumination to all mankind, flooding all souls with Divine Radiance, conveying the blessings of God's Mercy to the whole world. The earth, without the medium of the warmth and light of the rays of the sun, could receive no benefits from the sun.

Likewise the Holy Spirit is the very cause of the life of man; without the Holy Spirit he would have no intellect, he would be unable to acquire his scientific knowledge by which his great influence over the rest of creation is gained. The illumination of the Holy Spirit gives to man the power of thought, and enables him to make discoveries by which he bends the laws of nature to his will.

The Holy Spirit it is which, through the mediation of the Prophets of God, teaches spiritual virtues to man and enables him to attain Eternal Life.

All these blessings are brought to man by the Holy Spirit; therefore we can understand that the Holy Spirit is the Intermediary between the Creator and the created. The light and heat of the sun cause the earth to be fruitful, and create life in all things that grow; and the Holy Spirit quickens the souls of men.[28]

The light of the sun becomes apparent in each object according to the capacity of that object. The difference is simply one of degree and receptivity. The stone would be a recipient only to a limited extent; another created thing might be as a mirror wherein the sun is fully reflected; but the same light shines upon both.

The most important thing is to polish the mirrors of hearts in order that they may become illumined and receptive of the divine light. One heart may possess the capacity of the polished mirror; another, be covered and obscured by the dust and dross of this world. Although the same Sun is shining upon both, in the mirror which is polished, pure and sanctified you may behold the Sun in all its fullness, glory and power, revealing its majesty and effulgence; but in the mirror which is rusted and obscured there is no capacity for reflection, although so far as the Sun itself is concerned it is shining thereon and is neither lessened nor deprived. Therefore, our duty lies in seeking to polish the mirrors of our hearts in order that we shall become reflectors of that light and recipients of the divine bounties which may be fully revealed through them.[29]

Man possesses two kinds of susceptibilities: the natural emotions, which are like dust upon the mirror, and spiritual susceptibilities, which are merciful and heavenly characteristics.

There is a power which purifies the mirror from dust and transforms its reflection into intense brilliancy and radiance so that spiritual susceptibilities may chasten the hearts and heavenly bestowals sanctify them. What is the dust which obscures the mirror? It is attachment to the world, avarice, envy, love of luxury and comfort, haughtiness and self-desire; this is the dust which prevents reflection of the rays of the Sun of Reality in the mirror. The natural emotions are blameworthy and are like rust which deprives the heart of the bounties of God. But sincerity, justice, humility, severance, and love for the believers of God will purify the mirror and make it radiant with reflected rays from the Sun of Truth.

It is my hope that you may consider this matter, that you may search out your own imperfections and not think of the imperfections of anybody else. Strive with all your power to be free from imperfections. Heedless souls are always seeking faults in others. What can the hypocrite know of others' faults when he is blind to his own? . . . As long as a man does not find his own faults, he can never become perfect. Nothing is more fruitful for man than the knowledge of his own shortcomings. The Blessed Perfection says, "I wonder at the man who does not find his own imperfections."[30]

The Meaning of Suffering

Grieve not because of my imprisonment and calamity; for this prison is my beautiful garden, my mansioned paradise, and my throne of dominion among mankind. My calamity in my prison is a crown to me in which I glory among the righteous.[31]

On the way back the evening light was waning as we

crossed the Serpentine bridge. Rows of shining lamps beneath the trees, stretching as far as our eyes could see into the distance, made that part of London into a glowing fairyland.

"I am very much pleased with this scene. Light is good, most good. There was much darkness in the prison at 'Akká," said the Master.

Our hearts were sad as we thought on those somber years within that dismal fortress, where the only light was in the indomitable spirit of the Master Himself! When we said: "We are glad, oh! so full of gladness that you are free," He said: "Freedom is not matter of place, but of condition. It was happy in that prison, for those days were passed in the path of service.

"To me prison was freedom.

"Troubles are a rest to me.

"Death is life.

"To be despised is honor.

"Therefore was I full of happiness all through that prison time.

"When one is released from the prison of self, that is indeed freedom! For self is the greatest prison.

"When this release takes place, one can never be imprisoned. Unless one accepts dire vicissitudes, not with dull resignation, but with radiant acquiescence, one cannot attain this freedom."[32]

❈

Grief and sorrow do not come to us by chance, they are sent to us by the Divine Mercy for our own perfecting.

While a man is happy he may forget his God; but when grief comes and sorrows overwhelm him, then will he remember his Father who is in Heaven, and who is able to deliver him from his humiliations.

Men who suffer not, attain no perfection. The plant most pruned by the gardeners is that one which, when the summer comes, will have the most beautiful blossoms and the most abundant fruit.

The laborer cuts up the earth with his plough, and from that earth comes the rich and plentiful harvest. The more a man is chastened, the greater is the harvest of spiritual virtues shown forth by him.[33]

❈

It is clear, then, that tests and trials are, for sanctified souls, but God's bounty and grace, while to the weak, they are a calamity, unexpected and sudden.

These tests . . . do but cleanse the spotting of self from off the mirror of the heart, till the Sun of Truth can cast its rays thereon; for there is no veil more obstructive than the self, and however tenuous that veil may be, at the last it will completely shut a person out, and deprive him of his portion of eternal grace.[34]

The mystery of sacrifice is a profound one, requiring detailed explanation. But briefly it may be stated that sacrificial love is the love shown by the moth towards the candle, by the parched wayfarer towards the living fountain, by the true lover towards his beloved, by the yearning heart towards the goal of its desire.

The sacrificial lover, in other words, should become entirely forgetful of self, enthralled by the Beloved, enamored of His countenance, and enraptured by His locks. Utterly unmindful of body, soul, life, comfort, and existence, he should seek the good pleasure of the True One, desire to gaze upon His countenance, and wish to follow in His way. Inebriated by the cup He proffereth and submissive in His hands, he should become completely oblivious of his own existence so that, like unto the light of truth, he may shine forth from the horizon of eternity. This is the first degree of sacrifice.

As for the second degree, it is in man's becoming rid of all attachment to the human world and finding deliverance from the darkness of the contingent realm. In this degree, the radiance of the All-Merciful should so suffuse and permeate his being that this nether world may pale into non-existence before the reality of the

Kingdom. When a lump of iron is cast into the forge, its ferrous qualities of blackness, coldness, and solidity, which symbolize the attributes of the human world, are concealed and disappear, while the fire's distinctive qualities of redness, heat, and fluidity, which symbolize the virtues of the Kingdom, become visibly apparent in it, so that the iron may be said to have acquired the virtues of that element. Even so is it with man: when, released from earthly bonds, from human imperfections, and from the darkness of the animal world, he setteth foot within the realm of the unbounded, partaketh of the outpourings of the unseen world, and acquireth divine virtues and perfections, then will he become a sacrificial lover of the Sun of Truth, and make haste with heart and soul to reach the place of sacrifice.[35]

Prayer

O thou daughter of the Kingdom!

Know thou that prayer and supplication are the water of life; through them one's being is quickened and one's soul refreshed and gladdened. Do thou persevere therein as far as thou art able, and recommend to others likewise to engage in prayer and supplication.[36]

Thou hast asked what shouldst thou do and what prayer shouldst thou offer in order to become informed of the mysteries of God. Pray thou with an attracted heart and supplicate thou with a spirit stirred by the glad tidings of God. Then the doors of the kingdom of mysteries shall be opened before thy face and thou shalt comprehend the realities of all things.[37]

There is nothing sweeter in the world of existence than prayer.

Man must live in a state of prayer. The most blessed condition is the condition of prayer and supplication. Prayer is conversation with God. The greatest attainment or the sweetest state is none other than conversation with God. It creates spirituality, creates mindfulness and celestial feelings, begets new attractions of the Kingdom and engenders the susceptibilities of the higher intelligence. The highest attribute given to his holiness Moses is the following verse: "God carried along a conversation with Moses."

What is prayer? It is conversation with God. While man prays he sees himself in the presence of God. If he concentrates his attention he will surely at the time of prayer realize that he is conversing with God. Often at night I do not sleep, and the thoughts of this world weigh heavily on my mind. I toss uneasily in my bed. Then in the darkness of the night I get up and pray—converse with God. It is most sweet and uplifting.

Prayer and supplication are so effective that they inspire one's heart for the whole day with high ideals and supreme sanctity and calmness. One's heart must be sensitive to the music of prayer. He must feel the effect of prayer. He must not be like an organ from which softest notes stream forth without having consciousness of sensation in itself.[38]

Prayer and supplication are two wings whereby man soars toward the heavenly mansion of the True One. However, verbal repetition of prayer does not suffice. One must live in a continual attitude of prayer. When man is spiritually free his mind becomes the altar of prayer and his heart the sanctity of prayer. Then the meaning of the verse, "We will lift up from before his eyes the veil," will become fulfilled in him.[39]

When asked if prayer was necessary since presumably

God knows the wishes of all our hearts Abdul-Baha said:

"If one friend feels love for another he will wish to say so. Though he knows that the friend is aware that he loves him, he will still wish to say so. If there is anyone that you love do you not seek an opportunity to speak with him, to speak lovingly with him, to bring him gifts, to write him letters? If you do not feel such a desire it would be that you did not love your friend. God knows the wishes of all hearts. But the impulse to pray is a natural one springing from man's love to God.

"If there be no love, if there be no pleasure or spiritual enjoyment in prayer, do not pray. Prayer should spring from love, from the desire of the person to commune with God. Just as the lover never ceases from wishing to communicate with the beloved so does the lover of God always wish for constant communication with the Deity.

"Prayer need not be in words, but in thought and attitude. But if this love and this desire are lacking it i[s] useless to try to force them. Words without love me[an] nothing. If a person talks to you as an unpleasant d[uty] with no love or pleasure in his meeting with you [do] you wish to converse with him? Efforts should [be] made to make attachment to God."[40]

The prayerful attitude is attained by two means. Just as a man who is going to deliver a lecture prepares therefor and his preparation consists of certain meditations and notations, so the preparation for the prayerful attitude is detaching one's mind from all other thoughts save the thought of God at the time of prayer and then praying when the prayerful attitude shall be attained.[41]

Automatic, formalistic prayers which do not touch the core of the heart are of no avail. How sweet, how delicious, how satisfying, how spiritual is prayer in the middle of the night! While all the eyes are closed the eyes of the worshipper are wide open. While all the ears are stopped the ears of the suppliant are attuned to the subtle music of God. While the majority of the people are fast asleep the adorer of the Ideal Beloved is wakeful. All around him there is a rare and delicate silence, deep, airy, ethereal silence, calm, magical and subtle—and there is the worshipper, communing with nature and the author of nature.[42]

Prayer For Intimacy with God

O Lord, my God and my Haven in my distress! My Shield and my Shelter in my woes! My Asylum and

Refuge in time of need and in my loneliness my Companion! In my anguish my Solace, and in my solitude a loving Friend! The Remover of the pangs of my sorrows and the Pardoner of my sins!

Wholly unto Thee do I turn, fervently imploring Thee with all my heart, my mind and my tongue, to shield me from all that runs counter to Thy will in this, the cycle of Thy divine unity, and to cleanse me of all defilement that will hinder me from seeking, stainless and unsullied, the shade of the tree of Thy grace.

Have mercy, O Lord, on the feeble, make whole the sick, and quench the burning thirst.

Gladden the bosom wherein the fire of Thy love doth smolder, and set it aglow with the flame of Thy celestial love and spirit.

Robe the tabernacles of divine unity with the vesture of holiness, and set upon my head the crown of Thy favor.

Illumine my face with the radiance of the orb of Thy bounty, and graciously aid me in ministering at Thy holy threshold.

Make my heart overflow with love for Thy creatures and grant that I may become the sign of Thy mercy, the token of Thy grace, the promoter of concord amongst Thy loved ones, devoted unto Thee, uttering Thy commemoration and forgetful of self but ever mindful of what is Thine.

O God, my God! Stay not from me the gentle gales of Thy pardon and grace and deprive me not of the wellsprings of Thine aid and favor.

'Neath the shade of Thy protecting wings let me nestle, and cast upon me the glance of Thine all-protecting eye.

Loose my tongue to laud Thy name amidst Thy people, that my voice may be raised in great assemblies and from my lips may stream the flood of Thy praise.

Thou art, in all truth, the Gracious, the Glorified, the Mighty, the Omnipotent.[43]

Prayer to be recited at Midnight

O seeker of Truth! If thou desirest that God may open thine eye, thou must supplicate unto God, pray to and commune with Him at midnight, saying:

O Lord, I have turned my face unto Thy kingdom of oneness and am immersed in the sea of Thy mercy. O Lord, enlighten my sight by beholding Thy lights in this dark night, and make me happy by the wine of Thy love in this wonderful age. O Lord, make me hear Thy call, and open before my face the doors of Thy heaven, so that I may see the light of Thy glory and become attracted to Thy beauty.

Verily, Thou art the Giver, the Generous, the Merciful, the Forgiving.[44]

Prayer for Those Who Have Passed On

Those who have ascended have different attributes from those who are still on earth, yet there is no real separation. In prayer there is a mingling of station, a mingling of condition. Pray for them as they pray for you.[45]

Someone present asked how it was that in prayer and meditation the heart often turns with instinctive appeal to some friend who has passed into the next life.

Abdul-Baha answered: "It is a law of God's creation that the weak should lean upon the strong. Those to whom you turn may be mediators of God's power to you, even as when on earth. But it is the one Holy Spirit which strengthens all men."[46]

O my God! O Thou forgiver of sins! Bestower of gifts! Dispeller of afflictions!

Verily, I beseech Thee to forgive the sins of such as have abandoned the physical garment and have ascended to the spiritual world.

O my Lord! Purify them from trespasses, dispel their sorrows, and change their darkness into light. Cause them to enter the garden of happiness, cleanse

them with the most pure water, and grant them to
behold Thy splendors on the loftiest mount.[47]

Service is Prayer

. . . when thy fingers grasp the paint brush, it is as if
thou wert at prayer in the Temple.[48]

❀

Briefly, all effort and exertion put forth by man from the
fullness of his heart is worship, if it is prompted by the
highest motives and the will to do service to humanity.
This is worship: to serve mankind and to minister to the
needs of the people. Service is prayer. A physician
ministering to the sick, gently, tenderly, free from
prejudice and believing in the solidarity of the human
race, he is giving praise.[49]

❀

. . . In accordance with the divine teachings the acquisition of sciences and the perfection of arts are considered acts of worship. If a man engageth with all his
power in the acquisition of a science or in the perfection of an art, it is as if he has been worshipping God
in churches and temples. . . . What bounty greater than

53

this: that science should be considered as an act of
worship and art as service to the Kingdom of God.[50]

A workman who had left his bag of tools in the hall was
welcomed with smiling kindness by 'Abdu'l-Bahá. With
a look of sadness the man said: "I don't know much
about religious things, as I have no time for anything
but my work."

"That is well. Very well. A day's work done in the
spirit of service is in itself an act of worship. Such work
is a prayer unto God."

The man's face cleared from its shadow of doubt
and hesitation, and he went out from the Master's
presence happy and strengthened, as though a weighty
burden had been taken away.[51]

Meditation

It is an axiomatic fact that while you meditate you are
speaking with your own spirit. In that state of mind
you put certain questions to your spirit and the spirit
answers: the light breaks forth and the reality is revealed . . . .Through the faculty of meditation man
attains to eternal life; through it he receives the breath

of the Holy Spirit—the bestowal of the Spirit is given in reflection and meditation.

The spirit of man is itself informed and strengthened during meditation; through it affairs of which man knew nothing are unfolded before his view. Through it he receives Divine inspiration, through it he receives heavenly food.

Meditation is the key for opening the doors of mysteries. In that state man abstracts himself: in that state man withdraws himself from all outside objects; in that subjective mood he is immersed in the ocean of spiritual life and can unfold the secrets of things-in-themselves. To illustrate this, think of man as endowed with two kinds of sight; when the power of insight is being used the outward power of vision does not see.

This faculty of meditation frees man from the animal nature, discerns the reality of things, puts man in touch with God.

This faculty brings forth from the invisible plane the sciences and arts. Through the meditative faculty inventions are made possible, colossal undertakings are carried out; through it governments can run smoothly. Through this faculty man enters into the very Kingdom of God.

Neverthelsss some thoughts are useless to man; they are like waves moving in the sea without results.

But if the faculty of meditation is bathed in the inner light and characterized with divine attributes, the results will be confirmed.

The meditative faculty is akin to the mirror; if you put it before earthly objects it will reflect them. Therefore if the spirit of man is contemplating earthly subjects he will be informed of these.

But if you turn the mirror of your spirits heavenwards, the heavenly constellations and the rays of the Sun of Reality will be reflected in your hearts, and the virtues of the Kingdom will be obtained.

Therefore let us keep this faculty rightly directed—turning it to the heavenly Sun and not to earthly objects—so that we may discover the secrets of the Kingdom, and comprehend the allegories of the Bible and the mysteries of the spirit.

May we indeed become mirrors reflecting the heavenly realities, and may we become so pure as to reflect the stars of heaven.[52]

Verily, I assure thee that if thy heart be freed from every thought and mention and thy soul drawn wholly towards God's Kingdom; if thou forgettest all save Him and consortest with His Spirit, then shall the Spirit confirm thee with a power that penetrateth all things, with a light that illuminateth all regions, and with a brilliant flame that mounteth up unto the highest heaven, and apprise thee of those universal truths and divine teachings of which thou hadst no knowledge.[53]

Invocation

'Abdu'l-Bahá teaches how the practice of invocation or repetition of "the Greatest Name" (*Alláh'u'Abhá*, God is Most Glorious) leads to union with God, illumination and spiritual rebirth. The use of invocation is well developed among the mystics of Islam, the Sufis. The repetition of sacred phrases is called *dhikr* (pronounced zikr, meaning remembrance). This spiritual practice of invocation is praised by 'Abdu'l-Bahá. He encouraged spiritual seekers to "recite the Greatest Name at every morn, and (to) turn . . . unto the kingdom of Abhá, until though mayest apprehend the mysteries."[54]

Through the invocation of the Greatest Name, 'Abdu'l-Bahá maintains that "the doors of the kingdom of God open, illumination is vouchsafed and divine union results. . . .The use of the Greatest Name, and dependence upon it, causes the soul to strip itself of the husks

of mortality and to step forth freed, reborn, a new
creature."[55]

'Abdu'l-Bahá encourages the use of the sacred phrase
Alláh'u'Abhá as a focus for invocation: "The Greatest
Name should be found upon the lips in the first awak-
ening moment of early dawn. It should be fed upon by
constant use in daily invocation, in trouble, under
opposition, and should be the last word breathed when
the head rests upon the pillow at night. It is the name of
comfort, protection, happiness, illumination, love and
unity."[56]

Beware! Beware!

Beware lest ye harm any soul, or make any heart to
sorrow; lest ye wound any man with your words, be he
known to you or a stranger, be he friend or foe. Pray ye
for all; ask ye that all be blessed, all be forgiven.

Beware, beware, lest any of you seek vengeance,
even against one who is thirsting for your blood.
Beware, beware, lest ye offend the feelings of another,
even though he be an evil-doer, and he wish you ill.
Look ye not upon the creatures, turn ye to their Creator. See ye not the never-yielding people, see but the

Lord of Hosts. Gaze ye not down upon the dust, gaze upward at the shining sun, which hath caused every patch of darksome earth to glow with light.[57]

In accordance with the divine teachings in this glorious dispensation we should not belittle anyone and call him ignorant, saying: 'You know not, but I know'. Rather, we should look upon others with respect, and when attempting to explain and demonstrate, we should speak as if we are investigating the truth, saying: 'Here these things are before us. Let us investigate to determine where and in what form the truth can be found.' The teacher should not consider himself as learned and others ignorant. Such a thought breedeth pride, and pride is not conducive to influence. The teacher should not see in himself any superiority; he should speak with the utmost kindliness, lowliness and humility, for such speech exerteth influence and educateth the souls.[58]

In all of my many opportunities of meeting, of listening to and talking with 'Abdu'l-Bahá, I was impressed, and constantly more deeply impressed, with His method of teaching souls. That is the word. He did not attempt to reach the mind alone. He sought the soul, the reality of every one He met. Oh, He could be logical, even scientific in His presentation of an argument, as He demonstrated constantly in the many addresses I have heard Him give and the many more I have read. But it was not the logic of the schoolman, not the science of the class room. His lightest word, His slightest association with a soul was shot through with an illuminating radiance which lifted the hearer to a higher plane of consciousness. Our hearts burned within us when He spoke. And He never argued, of course. Nor did He press a point. He left one free. There was never an assumption of authority, rather He was ever the personification of humility. He taught "as if offering a gift to a king." He never told me what I should do, beyond suggesting that what I was doing was right. Nor did He ever tell me what I should believe. He made Truth and Love so beautiful and royal that the heart perforce did reverence. He showed me by His voice, manner, bearing, smile, how I should be, knowing that out of the pure soil of being the good fruit of deeds and words would surely spring.[59]

You must manifest complete love and affection toward

all mankind. Do not exalt yourselves above others, but consider all as your equals, recognizing them as the servants of one God. Know that God is compassionate toward all; therefore, love all from the depths of your hearts, prefer all religionists before yourselves, be filled with love for every race and be kind toward the people of all nationalities. Never speak disparagingly of others, but praise without distinction. Pollute not your tongues by speaking evil of another. Recognize your enemies as friends, and consider those who wish you evil as the wishers of good. You must not see evil as evil and then compromise with your opinion, for to treat in a smooth, kindly way one whom you consider evil or an enemy is hypocrisy, and this is not worthy or allowable. You must consider your enemies as your friends, look upon your evil-wishers as your well-wishers and treat them accordingly. Act in such a way that your heart may be free from hatred. Let not your heart be offended with anyone. If some one commits an error and wrong toward you, you must instantly forgive him. Do not complain of others. Refrain from reprimanding them, and if you wish to give admonition or advice, let it be offered in such a way that it will not burden the bearer. Turn all your thoughts toward bringing joy to hearts. Beware! Beware! lest ye offend any heart.[60]

'Abdu'l-Bahá

One day [in London] a woman asked to be permitted to see the Master.

"Have you an appointment?"

"Alas! No."

"I am sorry," answered the over-zealous friend who met her in the hall, "but He is occupied now with most important people, and cannot be disturbed."

The woman turned away, feeling too humble to persist in her appeal, but, oh! so bitterly disappointed. Before she had reached the foot of the stairway, she was overtaken by a breathless messenger from 'Abdu'l-Bahá.

"He wishes to see you, come back! He has told me to bring you to Him."

We had heard his voice from the door of His audience room speaking with authority: "A heart has been hurt. Hasten, hasten, bring her to me!" [61]

III

A Simple Life

Contentment

How complex is the life of the present age and how much more complex we are making it daily! The needs of humanity seem never to come to an end. The more men accumulate the more they want. There is only one way of freedom and that is by shutting one's eyes and heart to all these things which distract the mind.[62]

Let nothing grieve thee, and be thou angered at none. It behooves thee to be content with the Will of God.[63]

✳

Be thou not unhappy; the tempest of sorrow shall pass;
regret will not last; disappointment will vanish; the fire
of the love of God will become enkindled, and the
thorns and briars of sadness and despondency will be
consumed![64]

✳

Grieve not over the troubles and hardships of this
nether world, nor be glad in times of ease and comfort,
for both shall pass away. This present life is even as a
swelling wave, or a mirage, or drifting shadows.[65]

✳

In this world we are influenced by two sentiments: joy
and pain. . . . There is no human being untouched by
these two influences; but all the sorrow and the grief
that exist come from the world of matter—the spiritual
world bestows only joy![66]

✳

One who is imprisoned by desires is always unhappy;
the children of the Kingdom have unchained themselves from their desires. Break all fetters and seek for

'Abdu'l-Bahá and child at
Green Acre, Maine, 1912.

spiritual joy and enlightenment; then, though you walk on this earth, you will perceive yourselves to be within the divine horizon.[67]

Anyone can live contentedly in circumstances of ease and comfort, health and well-being, gratification and felicity; but to remain happy and contented in the face of difficulty, hardship, and the onslaught of disease and sickness—this is an indication of nobility.[68]

Man must live in contentment with the conditions of his time. He must not make himself the slave of any habit. He must eat a piece of stale bread with the same relish and enjoyment as the most sumptuous dinner. Contentment is real wealth. If one develops within himself the quality of contentment he will become independent. Contentment is the creator of happiness. When one is contented he does not care either for riches or poverty. He lives above the influence of them and is indifferent to them. When we were in Baghdad often with one pound of meat we served dinner to fifteen or twenty people. We cooked with it Persian stew and filled the pot with water so everyone could have a bowl of thin soup. Notwithstanding this we were all very happy and thought that ours was the most delicious dinner.[69]

A man may be absolutely poor and dispossessed of everything, and yet be worldly. Another man may be very wealthy and yet severed. Severance means that one's heart must not be attached to the things of this world. It does not mean that a man must dispossess himself of them, or that he must not work and earn or practice his profession, whatever it may be, in the world. It does not mean that he must not put on what he has. If he has a silk garb, let him wear that; and if he has not, but has a suit of cotton goods, let him wear that clean. He must feel the same in both.[70]

The Master kept little clothing—one coat at a time was ample. He ate little food. He was known to begin His day with tea, goat's milk cheese and wheat bread. And at the evening meal a cup of milk and a piece of bread might suffice. He considered the latter a healthy meal. . . . 'Abdu'l-Bahá's sparse diet also included herbs and olives—it rarely included meat.[71]

✦

Often his friends in Persia . . . send ['Abdu'l-Bahá] costly garments. These he wears once, out of respect for the sender; then he gives them away.

A few months ago this happened: The wife of the Master was about to depart on a journey. Fearing that her husband would give away his cloak and so be left without one for himself, she left a second cloak with her daughter, charging her not to inform her father of it. Not long after her departure, the Master, suspecting, it would seem, what had been done, said to his daughter, "Have I another cloak?" The daughter could not deny it, but told her father of her mother's charge. The Master replied, "How could I be happy having two cloaks knowing that there are those that have none?" Nor would he be content until he had given the second cloak away.[72]

✦

The mind of a contented person is always peaceful and his heart is at rest. He is like a monarch ruling over the whole world. How happily such a man helps himself to his frugal meals. How joyfully he takes his walks and how peacefully he sleeps![73]

Prayer for Contentment

O God, my God! Thou seest me, Thou knowest me; Thou art my Haven and my Refuge. None have I sought nor any will I seek save Thee; no path have I trodden not any will I tread but the path of Thy love. In the dark-some night of despair, my eye turneth expectant and full of hope to the morn of Thy boundless favor and at the hour of dawn my drooping soul is refreshed and strengthened in remembrance of Thy beauty and perfection. He who the grace of Thy mercy aideth, though he be but a drop, shall become the boundless ocean, and the merest atom which the outpouring Thy loving-kindness assisteth, shall shine even as the radiant star.[74]

Spiritual Food

The spiritual food is the principal food, whereas the physical food is not so important. The effect of the spiritual food is eternal. Through the material food the body exists, but through the spiritual food the spirit will be nourished. The material food, that is, the food for the body, is simply water and bread, but the food for the intellect is knowledge and the food for the spirit is the significances of the Heavenly Words and the bounties of the Holy Spirit.[75]

That which is most delicious in the world of existence is love. The air of itself is not delicious, neither is water, nor in short, all the elements; but when coupled with love it is most delicious. Love is the best condiment. When Love exists in the heart the slightest gesture proves welcome. When love exists in the heart, even if it be a stripe it is delicious.

For instance: the food on this table is nothing, indeed very simple; yet because it is prompted by Love it is delicious.

The Lord's Supper of Christ was indeed a very common thing, but because there was excessive Love among the individual members who convened there, that table surpassed the royal tables, and it was established as the Lord's Supper. Even now, at this time, it is known as such. This was due to the Love which existed between Jesus Christ and the disciples.[76]

Body and Soul

There are two ways of healing sickness, material means and spiritual means. The first is by the treatment of physicians; the second consisteth in prayers offered by the spiritual ones to God and in turning to Him. Both means should be used and practised.

Illnesses which occur by reason of physical causes should be treated by doctors with medical remedies; those which are due to spiritual causes disappear through spiritual means. Thus an illness caused by affliction, fear, nervous impressions, will be healed more effectively by spiritual rather than by physical treatment. Hence, both kinds of treatment should be followed; they are not contradictory. Therefore thou shouldst also accept physical remedies inasmuch as these too have come from the mercy and favor of God, Who hath revealed and made manifest medical science so that His servants may profit from this kind of treatment also. Thou shouldst give equal attention to spiritual treatments, for they produce marvellous effects.

Now, if thou wishest to know the true remedy which will heal man from all sickness and will give him the health of the divine kingdom, know that it is the precepts and teachings of God. Focus thine attention upon them.[77]

'Abdu'l-Bahá said:—"There is but one power which heals—that is God. The state or condition through which the healing takes place is the confidence of the heart. By some this state is reached through pills, powders, and physicians. By others through hygiene, fast-ing, and prayer; by others through direct perception."

On another occasion 'Abdu'l-Bahá said with regard to the same subject, "All that we see around us is the work of mind. It is mind in the herb and in the mineral that acts on the human body, and changes its condition."[78]

We should all visit the sick. When they are in sorrow and suffering, it is a real help and benefit to have a friend come. Happiness is a great healer to those who are ill. In the East it is the custom to call upon the patient often and meet him individually. The people in the East show the utmost kindness and compassion to the sick and suffering. This has greater effect than the remedy itself. You must always have this thought of love and affection when you visit the ailing and afflicted.[79]

Often when the family of Abdul-Baha was about to sit down to dinner at night, the report would come of some unfortunate who was starving, and who had been overlooked in the visits of the day. Then quickly the hot appetizing meal would be bundled into a basket, and rushed away to the suffering family, while Abdul-Baha would smile and say, "It does not matter for us, we had dinner last night, we shall have dinner tomorrow!"

Often he sent his bed to a feverish invalid whom he discovered, because it required thirty-six hours at least to procure a bed from Haifa, the nearest point of supply, and Abdul-Baha would be perfectly comfortable wrapped in a blanket, and lying upon the floor of his room, or the roof of the house, while he would not have been able to sleep at all, conscious of a bedless invalid, feverish and pain racked. He could not endure the sight of suffering which he was able to relieve.[80]

The Spiritual Path

Know, O thou possessors of insight, that true spirituality is like unto a lake of clear water which reflects the divine. . . There is another kind which is like a mirage, seeming to be spiritual when it is not. That which is truly spiritual must light the path to God, and must result in deeds. We cannot believe the call to be spiritual when there is no result. Spirit is reality, and when the spirit in each of us seeks to join itself with the Great Reality, it must in turn give life.[81]

All over the world one hears beautiful sayings extolled and noble precepts admired. All men say they love what is good, and hate everything that is evil! Sincerity is to be admired, whilst lying is despicable. Faith is a virtue, and treachery is a disgrace to humanity. It is a blessed thing to gladden the hearts of men, and wrong to be the cause of pain. To be kind and merciful is right, while to hate is sinful. Justice is a noble quality and injustice an iniquity. That it is one's duty to be pitiful and harm no one, and to avoid jealousy and malice at all costs. Wisdom is the glory of man, not ignorance; light, not darkness! It is a good thing to turn one's face toward God, and foolishness to ignore Him. That it is our duty to guide man upward, and not to mislead him and be the cause of his downfall. There are many more examples like unto these.

But all these sayings are but words and we see very few of them carried into the world of action. On the contrary, we perceive that men are carried away by passion and selfishness, each man thinking only of what will benefit himself even if it means the ruin of his brother. They are all anxious to make their fortune and care little or nothing for the welfare of others. They are concerned about their own peace and comfort, while the condition of their fellows troubles them not at all.

Unhappily this is the road most men tread.[82]

To live the life is:

To be no cause of grief to anyone.

To be kind to all people and to love them with a pure spirit.

Should opposition or injury happen to us, to bear it, to be as kind as ever we can be, and through all, to love the people. Should calamity exist in the greatest degree, to rejoice, for these things are the gifts and favors of God.

To be silent concerning the faults of others, to pray for them; and to help them, through kindness, to correct their faults.

To look always at the good and not at the bad. If a man has ten good qualities and one bad one, look at the ten and forget the one. And if a man has ten bad qualities and one good one, to look at the one and forget the ten.

Never to allow ourselves to speak one unkind word about another, even though that other be our enemy.

To do all of our deeds in kindness.

To sever our hearts from ourselves and from the world.

To be humble.

'Abdu'l-Bahá

To be servants of each other, and to know that we are less than anyone else.

To be as one soul in many bodies; for the more we love each other, the nearer we shall be to God; but to know that our love, our unity, our obedience must not be by confession, but of reality.

To act with cautiousness and wisdom.

To be truthful.

To be hospitable.

To be reverent.

To be a cause of healing for every sick one, a comforter for every sorrowing one, a pleasant water for every thirsty one, a heavenly table for every hungry one, a star to every horizon, a light for every lamp, a herald to everyone who yearns for the kingdom of God.[83]

Two things 'Abdu'l-Bahá taught her [Florence <u>Kh</u>ánum] she often quoted in Persian: One was that He said to her: *Sabr kun, mithl-e Man básh*—be patient, be as I am. The other was when some one expressed discouragement to Him, saying they could not possibly acquire all the qualities and virtues that Bahá'ís are directed to possess, and the Master replied: *Kam kam. Rúz bih rúz*—little by little; day by day.[84]

Oh, friends of God! If ye will trust in the Word of God and be strong; if ye will follow the precepts of Bahá'u'lláh to tend the sick, raise the fallen, care for the poor and needy, give shelter to the destitute, protect the oppressed, comfort the sorrowful and love the world of humanity with all your hearts, then I say unto you that ere long this meeting-place will see a wonderful harvest. Day by day each member will advance and become more and more spiritual. But ye must have a firm foundation and your aims and ambitions must be clearly understood by each member. They shall be as follows:

1. To show compassion and goodwill to all mankind.

2. To render service to humanity.

3. To endeavor to guide and enlighten those in darkness.

4. To be kind to everyone, and show forth affection to every living soul.

5. To be humble in your attitude towards God, to be constant in prayer to Him, so as to grow daily nearer to God.

6. To be so faithful and sincere in all your actions that every member may be known as embodying the qualities of honesty, love, faith, kindness, generosity,

and courage. To be detached from all that is not God,
attracted by the Heavenly Breath—a divine soul; so
that the world may know that a Bahá'í is a perfect
being. . . .

I pray to God that daily ye may advance in spirituality, that God's love may be more and more manifested
in you, that the thoughts of your hearts may be purified,
and that your faces may be ever turned towards Him.
May you one and all approach to the threshold of unity,
and enter into the Kingdom. May each of you be like
unto a flaming torch, lighted and burning bright with
the fire of the Love of God.[85]

We drove to a country inn [in Switzerland] where a
little later, after a walk, we were to have our tea. As the
Master stepped down from the car, about fifteen peasant
children with bunches of violets to sell closed in on
Him, formed a half circle around Him, holding up the
little purple bunches, raising their eyes to His Face with
grave astonishment. They pressed so close that they hid
Him below the waist, and the benediction in the look
He bent on them I shall never forget. Of course He
bought all the violets, drawing from His pocket hand-
fuls of francs. But when He had given to each child
bountifully, they held out their hands for more!

"Don't let them impose!" cried Laura.

"Tell them," said the Master very gently, "that they have taken.". . .

He turned and walked into the forest. . . .

We walked back to the inn through the woods, He leading us. As soon as He reappeared on the lawn of the inn the children again swarmed around Him, their hands still outstretched. Laura sternly ordered them off, for they were certainly imposing. "He would give away everything He has," she whispered to me. But the Master had discovered a tiny newcomer, a child much younger than the others, with a very sensitive face, who was looking wonderingly at Him.

"But," He said, "to this little one I have not given."
. . .

Again, when we left the inn, the children swarmed around the Master and gain Laura tried to save Him from their greediness.

"But here," said our Lord, "is a boy to whom I have not given."

"You gave to them all," said Laura.

"Call Hippolyte," ordered the Master. "I did not give to this boy, did I, Hippolyte?"

"I believe you did not."

Then the Master gave.[86]

'Abdu'l-Bahá in the Courtyard
of his home in Haifa, Palestine

IV

Unity

Universal Love and Fellowship

In every dispensation, there hath been the commandment of fellowship and love, but it was a commandment limited to the community of those in mutual agreement, not to the dissident foe. In this wondrous age, however, praised be God, the commandments of God are not delimited, not restricted to any one group of people, rather have all the friends been commanded to show forth fellowship and love, consideration and generosity and loving-kindness to every community on earth. Now must the lovers of God arise to carry out these instructions of His: let them be kindly fathers to the children of the human race, and compassionate brothers to the youth, and self-denying offspring to those bent with years. The meaning of this is that ye must show forth tenderness and love to every human being, even to your enemies, and welcome them all with unalloyed friendship, good cheer, and loving-kindness.[87]

Make haste to love! Make haste to trust! Make haste to give! To guidance come! Come ye for harmony! To behold the Star of Day!

Come here for kindliness, for ease! Come here for amity and peace!

Come and cast down your weapons of wrath, till unity is won! Come, and in the Lord's true path, each one help each one.[88]

I beg of God that ye will be bringers of joy, even as are the angels in heaven.[89]

O peoples of the world! The Sun of Truth hath risen to illumine the whole earth, and to spiritualize the community of man. Laudable are the results and the fruits thereof, abundant the holy evidences deriving from this grace. This is mercy unalloyed and purest bounty; it is light for the world and all its peoples; it is harmony and fellowship, and love and solidarity; indeed it is compassion and unity, and the end of foreignness; it is the being at one, in complete dignity and freedom, with all on earth.

The Blessed Beauty saith: 'Ye are all the fruits of one tree, the leaves of one branch.' Thus hath He likened this world of being to a single tree, and all its peoples to the leaves thereof, and the blossoms and fruits. It is needful for the bough to blossom, and leaf and fruit to flourish, and upon the interconnection of all parts of the world-tree, dependeth the flourishing of leaf and blossom, and the sweetness of the fruit.

For this reason must all human beings powerfully sustain one another and seek for everlasting life; and for this reason must the lovers of God in this contingent world become the mercies and the blessings sent forth by that clement King of the seen and unseen realms. Let them purify their sight and behold all humankind as leaves and blossoms and fruits of the tree of being. Let them at all times concern themselves with doing a

kindly thing for one of their fellows, offering to someone love, consideration, thoughtful help. Let them see
no one as their enemy, or as wishing them ill, but think
of all humankind as their friends; regarding the alien as
an intimate, the stranger as a companion, staying free of
prejudice, drawing no lines.

In this day, the one favored at the Threshold of the
Lord is he who handeth round the cup of faithfulness;
who bestoweth, even upon his enemies, the jewel of
bounty, and lendeth, even to his fallen oppressor, a
helping hand; it is he who will, even to the fiercest of
his foes, be a loving friend. These are the Teachings of
the Blessed Beauty, these the counsels of the Most Great
Name.[90]

O ye friends of God!

Show kindness unto all nations and peoples. Have
love for all, strive as far as ye are able to assuage men's
hearts, and make a mighty effort to bring cheer and
comfort to their souls. Be ye as the bounty of the cloud
unto the meadow, and the water of life unto the tree. Be
ye as a fragrant breath of musk in the nostrils of all
people, and a life-restoring breeze unto the sick. Be ye
as crystal water unto the thirsty, and a wise and knowl-
edgeable guide unto the erring. Be ye a kind and tender

parent unto the orphan, a most radiant and loving child unto the aged, and a princely treasure unto the destitute.

Regard ye love and fellowship as heavenly beatitude, and enmity and estrangement as infernal torment. Exert yourselves with heart and soul, forsake repose, make fervent supplication and entreaty, and implore God's grace and succor in order that ye may transform this nether world into the Abhá Paradise, and establish on this mortal plane the Most Exalted Kingdom. If ye be resolute in your endeavor it is certain that these lights will shine, that this bounteous cloud will rain, that this revitalizing breeze will blow, and that the exquisite fragrance of this musk will be diffused.[91]

It is incumbent upon everyone to show the utmost love, rectitude of conduct, straight forwardness and sincere kindliness unto all the peoples and kindreds of the world, be they friends or strangers. So intense must be the spirit of love and loving kindness, that the stranger may find himself a friend, the enemy a true brother, no difference whatsoever existing between them. For universality is of God and all limitations earthly. . . .

Wherefore, O my loving friends! Consort with all the peoples, kindreds and religions of the world with the utmost truthfulness, uprightness, faithfulness, kindliness, good-will and friendliness, that all the world of being may be filled with the holy ecstasy of the grace of Bahá, that ignorance, enmity, hate and rancor may vanish from the world and the darkness of estrangement amidst the peoples and kindreds of the world may give way to the Light of Unity.[92]

Rose Garden

This is a beautiful assembly. I am very happy that white and black are together. This is the cause of my happiness, for you all are the servants of one God and, therefore, brothers, sisters, mothers and fathers. In the sight of God there is no distinction between whites and blacks; all are as one. Anyone whose heart is pure is dear to God—whether white or black, red or yellow. Among the animals colors exist. The doves are white, black, red, blue; but notwithstanding this diversity of color they flock together in unity, happiness and fellowship, making no distinction among themselves, for they are all doves. Man is intelligent and thoughtful, endowed with powers of mind. Why, then, should he be influenced by distinction of color or race, since all belong to one human family? There is no sheep which shuns another as if saying, "I am white, and you are black." They graze together in completely unity, live together in fellowship and happiness. How then can man be limited and influenced by racial colors? The important thing is to realize that all are human, all are one progeny of Adam. Inasmuch as they are all one family, why should they be separated? . . .

Then it is evident that excellence does not depend upon color. Character is the true criterion of humanity. Anyone who possessed a good character, who has faith in God and is firm, whose actions are good, whose speech is good—that one is accepted at the threshold of God no matter what color he may be. In short— praise be to God!—you are the servants of God . . . My hope is that the white and the black will be united in perfect love and fellowship, with complete unity and brotherhood. Associate with each other, think of each other, and be like a rose garden. Anyone who goes into a rose garden will see various roses, white, pink, yellow, red, all growing together and replete with adornment. Each one accentuates the beauty of the other. Were all of one color, the garden would be monotonous to the eye. If they were all white or yellow or red, the garden would lack variety and attractiveness; but when the colors are varied, white, pink, yellow, red, there will be the greatest beauty. Therefore, I hope that you will be like a rose garden. Although different in colors, yet—

praise be to God!—you receive rays from the same sun. From one cloud the rain is poured upon you. You are under the training of one Gardener, and this Gardener is kind to all. Therefore, you must manifest the utmost kindness towards each other, and you may rest assured that whenever you are united, the confirmations of the Kingdom of Abhá will reach you, the heavenly favors will descend, the bounties of God will be bestowed, the Sun of Reality will shine, the cloud of mercy will pour its showers, and the breeze of divine generosity will waft its fragrances upon you.

I hope you will continue in unity and fellowship. How beautiful to see blacks and whites together! I hope, God willing, the day may come when I shall see the red men, the Indians, with you, also Japanese and others. Then there will be white roses, yellow roses, red roses, and a very wonderful rose garden will appear in the world.[93]

How unpleasing to the eye if all the flowers and plants, the leaves and blossoms, the fruits, the branches and the trees of that garden were all of the same shape and color! Diversity of hues, form and shape, enricheth and adorneth the garden, and heighteneth the effect thereof. In like manner, when divers shades of thought, temperament and character, are brought together under the power and influence of one central agency, the beauty and glory of human perfection will be revealed and made manifest. Naught but the celestial potency of the Word of God, which ruleth and transcendeth the realities of all things, is capable of harmonizing the divergent thoughts, sentiments, ideas, and convictions of the children of men. Verily, it is the penetrating power in all things, the mover of souls and the binder and regulator in the world of humanity.[94]

One Family

From every standpoint the world of humanity is undergoing a reformation. The laws of former governments and civilizations are in process of revision; scientific ideas and theories are developing and advancing to meet a new range of phenomena; invention and discovery are penetrating hitherto unknown fields, revealing new wonders and hidden secrets of the material universe; industries have vastly wider scope and production; everywhere the world of mankind is in the throes of evolutionary activity indicating the passing of the old conditions and advent of the new age of reformation. Old trees yield no fruitage; old ideas and methods are obsolete and worthless now. Old standards of ethics, moral codes and methods of living in the past will not suffice for the present age of advancement and progress.

This is the cycle of maturity and reformation in religion as well. Dogmatic imitations of ancestral beliefs are passing. They have been the axis around which religion revolved but now are no longer fruitful; on the contrary, in this day they have become the cause of human degradation and hindrance. Bigotry and dogmatic adherence to ancient beliefs have become the central and fundamental source of animosity among men, the obstacle to human progress, the cause of warfare and strife, the destroyer of peace, composure and welfare in the world. Consider conditions in the Balkans today: fathers mothers, children in grief and lamentation, the foundations of life overturned, cities laid waste and fertile lands made desolate by the ravages of war. These conditions are the outcome of hostility and hatred between nations and peoples of religion who imitate and adhere to the forms and violate the spirit and reality of the divine teachings.

While this is true and apparent, it is, likewise, evident that the Lord of mankind has bestowed infinite bounties upon the world in this century of maturity and consummation. The ocean of divine mercy is surging, the vernal showers are descending, the Sun of Reality is shining gloriously. Heavenly teachings applicable to the advancement in human conditions have been revealed in this merciful age. This reformation and renewal of the fundamental reality of religion constitute the true and outworking spirit of modernism, the unmistakable light of the world, the manifest effulgence of the Word of God, the divine remedy for all human ailment and the bounty of eternal life to all mankind.[95]

In cycles gone by, though harmony was established, yet, owing to the absence of means, the unity of all mankind could not have been achieved. Continents remained widely divided, nay even among the peoples of one and the same continent association and interchange of thought were well-nigh impossible. Consequently intercourse, understanding and unity amongst all the peoples and kindreds of the earth were unattainable. In this day, however, means of communication have multiplied, and the five continents of the earth have virtually merged into one. And for everyone it is now easy to travel to any land, to associate and exchange views with its peoples, and to become familiar, through publications, with the conditions, the religious beliefs and the thoughts of all men. In like manner all the members of the human family, whether peoples or governments, cities or villages, have become increasingly interdependent. For none is self-sufficiency any longer possible, inasmuch as political ties unite all peoples and nations, and the bonds of trade and industry, of agriculture and education, are being strengthened every day. Hence the unity of all mankind can in this day be achieved. Verily this is none other but one of the wonders of this wondrous age, this glorious century. Of this past ages have been deprived, for this century—the century of light—hath been endowed with unique and unprecedented glory, power and illumination. Hence the miraculous unfolding of a fresh marvel every day. Eventually it will be seen how bright its candles will burn in the assemblage of man.

Behold how its light is now dawning upon the world's darkened horizon. The first candle is unity in the political realm, the early glimmerings of which can now be discerned. The second candle is unity of thought in world undertakings, the consummation of which will ere long be witnessed. The third candle is unity in freedom which will surely come to pass. The fourth candle is unity in religion which is the corner-stone of the foundation itself, and which, by the power of God, will be revealed in all its splendor. The fifth candle is the unity of nations—a unity which in this century will be securely established, causing all the peoples of the world

to regard themselves as citizens of one common father-
land. The sixth candle is unity of races, making of all
that dwell on earth peoples and kindreds of one race.
The seventh candle is unity of language, i.e., the choice
of a universal tongue in which all peoples will be in-
structed and converse. Each and every one of these
will inevitably come to pass, inasmuch as the power
of the Kingdom of God will aid and assist in their
realization.[96]

Man should endeavor always to realize the Oneness of
Humanity. We are all children of God; all created by
God; all provided for by God and all under the protection of God. God is kind to all His children. Why
should they wage war between themselves? God is the
Real Shepherd—all are His sheep. There is no difference whatever among the members of the flock. He
educates all of us, is compassionate to all of us; protects
all of us. Ponder and you will understand that with the
bounties of God there is no restraint. His grace encom-
passes all mankind. All live under his bounty.[97]

'Abdu'l-Bahá

What profit is there in agreeing that universal friendship is good, and talking of the solidarity of the human race as a grand ideal? Unless these thoughts are translated into the world of action, they are useless. The wrong in the world continues to exist just because people talk only of their ideals, and do not strive to put them into practice. If actions took the place of words, the world's misery would very soon be changed into comfort.[98]

V

Renewal

Living the Golden Rule

Should other peoples and nations be unfaithful to you,
show your fidelity unto them; should they be unjust
toward you, show justice toward them; should they
keep aloof from you, attract them to yourselves; should
they show enmity, be friendly toward them; should they
poison your lives, sweeten their souls; should the inflict
a wound upon you, be a salve to their sores. Such are
the attributes of the sincere! Such are the attributes of
the faithful.[99]

❊

Ye must be brilliant lamps. Ye must shine as stars radiating love toward all mankind. May you be the cause of love amongst the nations. . . . Make peace with all the world. Love everybody; serve everybody. All are the servants of God. God has created all. He provideth for all. He is kind to all. Therefore, must we be kind to all.[100]

❊

In this day, the one favored at the Threshold of the Lord is he who handeth round the cup of faithfulness; who bestoweth, even upon his enemies, the jewel of bounty, and lendeth, even to his fallen oppressor, a helping hand; it is he who will, even to the fiercest of his foes, be a loving friend.[101]

The Season for Joy!

O ye friends of God!

Do ye know in what cycle ye are created and in what age ye exist? This is the age of the Blessed Perfection and this is the time of the Greatest Name! This is the century of the Manifestation, the age of the Sun of the horizons and the beautiful springtime of the Eternal One!

The earth is in motion and growth; the mountains, hills and prairies are green and pleasant; bounty is overflowing; mercy universal; rain is descending from the clouds of compassion; the brilliant sun is shining; the full moon adorneth the ethereal horizon; the great ocean-tide is flooding every little stream; the gifts and favors follow one upon the other and a refreshing breeze is blowing, wafting the fragrant perfume of the blossoms.

If we are not happy and joyous at this season, for what other season shall we wait and for what other time shall we look?

Boundless treasure is in the hand of the King of Kings! Lift the hem of thy garment to receive it.

This is the time for growing; the season for joyous gathering! Take the cup of the Testament in thy hand; leap and dance with ecstasy in the triumphal procession of the Covenant! Place your confidence in the everlasting bounty, turn to the presence of the generous God; ask assistance from the Kingdom of Abhá; seek confirmation from the Supreme World; turn thy vision to the horizon of eternal wealth; and pray for help from the Source of Mercy!

Soon shall ye see the friends attaining their longed-for destination and pitching their tents, while we are but in the first day of our journey.[102]

Soon the whole world, as in springtime, will change its garb. The turning and falling of the autumn leaves is past; the bleakness of the wintertime is over. The new year hath appeared and the spiritual springtime is at hand. The black earth is becoming a verdant garden; the deserts and mountains are teeming with red flowers; from the borders of the wilderness the tall grasses are standing like advance guards before the cypress and jessamine trees; while the birds are singing among the rose branches like the angels in the highest heavens, announcing the glad-tidings of the approach of that spiritual spring, and the sweet music of their voices is causing the real essence of all things to move and quiver.

O my spiritual friend! Dost thou know from what airs emanate the notes sung by those birds? They are from the melodies of peace and reconciliation, of love and unity, of justice and security, of concord and harmony. In a short time this heavenly singing will intoxicate all humanity; the foundations of enmity shall be destroyed; unity and affection shall be witnessed in every assembly; and the splendors of the love of God will shine forth in these great festivals.

Therefore, contemplate what a spirit of life God

hath given that the body of the whole earth may attain life everlasting! The Abhá Paradise will soon spread a pavilion in the midmost heart of the world, under whose shelter the beloved shall rejoice and the pure hearts shall repose in peace.[103]

Notes

Special acknowledgement and thanks to Peggy Caton, Ph.D., who worked on the early draft of this book. We are also grateful to the Research Department at the Bahá'í World Centre for their assistance in updating old translations.

[1] Browne, *A Traveller's Narrative*, Vol. 2, pp. xxxvi.

[2] Phelps, *Master in 'Akká*, pp. 2-4.

[3] Ibid., pp. 4-7.

[4] Esslemont, *Bahá'u'lláh and the New Era*, pp. 64-65.

[5] Phelps, *Master in 'Akká*, pp. 8, 10.

[6] Juliet Thompson, in *Star of the West*, Vol. 2 (November 23, 1911) no. 14, p. 9.

[7] From a newspaper article written by Wendell Phillips Dodge, a reporter for the New York City News Association, who interviewed 'Abdu'l-Bahá upon his arrival in America. Reprinted in *Star of the West*, Vol. 3 (April 28, 1912) no. 3, pp. 3-6.

[8] Brown, *Memories*, pp. 37-38.

[9] From Ford, "Economic Teaching," *Star of the West*, Vol. 8 (March 21, 1917) no. 1, pp. 4-5.

[10] From the table talks of 'Abdu'l-Bahá, collected by Laura Clifford Barney, 1904-1906, in *Some Answered Questions*, p. 233.

[11] From a talk given by 'Abdu'l-Bahá in Paris. November 10, 1912. In *Paris Talks*, pp. 88-90.

[12] From a talk given by 'Abdu'l-Bahá at the home of Madame Morey, Malden, Massachusetts. August 29, 1912. Notes by Edna McKinney. In *Promulgation of Universal Peace*, p. 294.

[13] Ibid., pp. 293-96.

[14] From a talk given by 'Abdu'l-Bahá at Green Acre, Maine. August 16, 1912. Notes by Edna McKinney. *Promulgation*, p. 255.

[15] From a talk given by 'Abdu'l-Bahá at the home of Mrs. Roberts, Denver, Colorado. September 24, 1912. *Promulgation*, p. 337.

[16] From a talk given by 'Abdu'l-Bahá at the Union Meeting of Advanced Thoughts Centers, New York. April 14, 1912. Ibid., p. 15.

[17] From *Selections from the Writings of 'Abdu'l-Bahá*, p. 37.

[18] Words of 'Abdu'l-Bahá; from *'Abdu'l-Bahá in London*, pp. 27-28

[19] Ibid., p. 95.

[20] From a talk given by 'Abdu'l-Bahá at the Church of the Ascension, New York. June 2, 1912. Notes by Esther Foster. *Promulgation*, p. 169.

[21] From a talk given by 'Abdu'l-Bahá in London. January 4, 1913. *Paris Talks*, p. 179.

[22] From a talk given by 'Abdu'l-Bahá in Paris. October 1912. Ibid., p. 17.

[23] From *Selections from the Writings of 'Abdu'l-Bahá*, p. 189.

[24] From the table talks of 'Abdu'l-Bahá, in *Some Answered Questions*, pp. 78-80.

[25] From *Selections from the Writings of 'Abdu'l-Bahá*, pp. 220-21.

[26] Ibid., p. 3.

[27] From a talk given by 'Abdu'l-Bahá to the Theosophical Society at the home of Mr. and Mrs. Arthur J. Parsons, Washington, D.C. Notes by Joseph H. Hannen. In *Promulgation*, pp. 59-60.

[28] From a talk given by 'Abdu'l-Bahá in Paris. October 31, 1912. In *Paris Talks*, p. 57-59.

[29] From a talk given by 'Abdu'l-Bahá at the Union Meeting of Advanced Thought Centers, Carnegie Lyceum, New York. April 14, 1912. Notes by Montford Mills and Howard MacNutt. In *Promulgation*, p. 14-15.

[30] From a talk given by 'Abdu'l-Bahá at the Hotel Victoria, Boston, Massachusetts. July 25, 1912. Notes by Edna McKinney. In *Promulgation*, p. 244.

[31] From a new translation provided by the Bahá'í World Center. Cf. *Tablets of Abdul-Baha*, Vol. 2, p. 258.

[32] From the memoirs of Lady Blomfield, *The Chosen Highway*, p. 166.

[33] From a talk given by 'Abdu'l-Bahá in Paris. October 27, 1912. In *Paris Talks*, pp. 50-51.

[34] From *Selections from the Writings of 'Abdu'l-Bahá*, p. 182.

[35] From a Tablet of 'Abdu'l-Bahá to an American Bahá'í, a new translation provided by the Bahá'í World Center. Cf. *Tablets of Abdul-Baha*, Vol. 2, pp. 354-55.

[36] From a new translation provided by the Bahá'í World Center. Cf. Notes of Miss Alma Albertson and other pilgrims, November and December, 1900. *Star of the West*, Vol. 8 (May

'Abdu'l-Bahá

17, 1917) no. 4, p. 42-43.

[37] Words of 'Abdu'l-Bahá from the Diary of Mirza Ahmad Sohrab, June 26, 1913. Ibid., p. 47.

[38] Ibid, p. 41.

[39] Ibid., pp. 41-42.

[40] Words of 'Abdu'l-Bahá quoted in an article in *The Fortnightly Review* (June 1911) by Miss E. S. Stevens. Ibid., p. 42.

[41] Words of 'Abdu'l-Bahá, quoted in Haney, *A Heavenly Feast*, p. 19.

[42] Words of 'Abdu'l-Bahá from the Diary of Mirza Ahmad Sohrab, September 3, 1914. *Star of the West*, ibid., p. 45.

[43] Prayer of 'Abdu'l-Bahá. quoted in *Bahá'í Prayers*, pp. 108-110.

[44] Prayer of 'Abdu'l-Bahá. Quoted in *Bahá'í Prayers*, p. 61-62.

[45] Words of 'Abdu'l-Bahá, quoted in *'Abdu'l-Bahá in London*, p. 96.

[46] Ibid., p. 97.

[47] Prayer of 'Abdu'l-Bahá, quoted in *Bahá'í Prayers*, p. 23.

[48] From a recently translated Tablet of 'Abdu'l-Bahá, "Extracts from the Writings and from Letters of the Guardian and the Universal House of Justice on the Arts and Architecture," p.2. Quoted in *The Creative Circle: Art, Literature, and Music in Bahá'í Perspective*, p. 61.

[49] From a talk given by 'Abdu'l-Bahá in London, December 26, 1912. Quoted in *Paris Talks*, pp. 176-77.

[50] From *Selections from the Writings of 'Abdu'l-Bahá*, pp. 144-45.

[51] From the memoirs of Lady Blomfield, *The Chosen Highway*, p. 152.

[52] From a talk given by 'Abdu'l-Bahá at the Friends'

Meeting House, London. January 12, 1913. Quoted in *Paris Talks*, pp. 174-76.

[53] From a new translation provided by the Bahá'í World Center. Cf. *Tablets of Abdul-Baha*, Vol. 3, pp. 706-707.

[54] "The Greatest Name, Symbol of the Cause", *Bahá'í News* (Oct. 1964), p. 2. Also see, Steven Scholl, "The Remembrance of God: An Invocation Technique in Sufism and the Writings of the Báb and Bahá'u'lláh," *Bahá'í Studies Bulletin* (1985).

[55] "The Greatest Name, Symbol of the Cause," ibid.

[56] Ibid.

[57] From *Selections from the Writings of 'Abdu'l-Bahá*, p. 73.

[58] Ibid., p. 30.

[59] From memoirs of Howard Colby Ives, *Portals to Freedom*, p. 39-40.

[60] From a talk given by 'Abdu'l-Bahá at the home of Mr. and Mrs. Edward B. Kinney, New York, December 2, 1912. Notes of Edna McKinney. *Promulgation*, p. 453.66.

[61] From the memoirs of Lady Blomfield, *The Chosen Highway*, pp. 158-59.

[62] Words of 'Abdu'l-Bahá, from the Diary of Ahmad Sohrab, September 21, 1913. *Star of the West*, Vol. 8 (April 9, 1917) no. 2, p. 17.

[63] From *Selections from the Writings of 'Abdu'l-Bahá*, p. 26.

[64] From *Tablets of Abdul-Baha Abbas*, vol. 3, p. 557.

[65] From *Selections from the Writings of 'Abdu'l-Bahá*, p. 177.

[66] From a talk given by 'Abdu'l-Bahá in Paris. November 22, 1912. *Paris Talks*, pp. 109-110.

[67] *'Abdu'l-Bahá in London*, p. 87.

[68] From a new translation provided by the Bahá'í World Center. Cf. *Tablets of Abdul-Baha*, Vol. 2, p. 263.

[69] Words of 'Abdu'l-Bahá, from the Diary of Mirza

Ahmad Sohrab, October 25, 1913. *Star of the West*, Vol. 8 (April 9, 1917) no. 2, p. 18.

[70] Words of 'Abdu'l-Bahá, quoted in Haney, *A Heavenly Feast*, p. 17.

[71] Honnold, *Vignettes*, p. 21.

[72] Phelps, *The Master in 'Akká*, p. 7.

[73] Words of 'Abdu'l-Bahá, from the Diary of Mirza Ahmad Sohrab, August 24, 1914. *Star of the West*, ibid.

[74] *Bahá'í Prayers*, pp. 31-32.

[75] Words of 'Abdu'l-Bahá at dinner, July 6, 1909, quoted in Thompson, *Diary*, p. 61.

[76] Words of 'Abdu'l-Bahá, quoted in Haney, *A Heavenly Feast*, p. 17.

[77] From *Selections from the Writings of 'Abdu'l-Bahá*, pp. 151-52.

[78] Words of 'Abdu'l-Bahá, quoted in *'Abdu'l-Bahá in London*, p. 95.

[79] From a talk given by 'Abdu'l-Bahá in New York, June 27, 1912. Notes by Emma C. Melick. *Promulgation*, p. 204.

[80] From Mary Hanford Ford, "The Economic Teaching of 'Abdu'l-Bahá," *Star of the West*, Vol. 8 (March 21, 1917) no. 1, p. 4.

[81] Words of 'Abdu'l-Bahá, from *'Abdu'l-Bahá in London*, p. 107.

[82] From a talk given by 'Abdu'l-Bahá in Paris, November 8, 1912. *Paris Talks*, pp. 79-80.

[83] Words of 'Abdu'l-Bahá, quoted in Townshend, *'Abdu'l-Bahá: The Master*, pp. 72-73.

[84] Memoir of Florence Khánum (Madame Ali Kuli Khan), in Gail, "Florence Breed Khanum," *The Bahá'í World*, Vol. 12, p. 704.

[85] From a lecture given by 'Abdu'l-Bahá in Paris, November 6, 1912. *Paris Talks*, pp. 73-74.

[86] From Thompson, *Diary*, August 25, 1912, pp. 174-76.

[87] Words of 'Abdu'l-Bahá, from *'Abdu'l-Bahá in London*, pp. 20-21.

[88] From *Selections from the Writings of 'Abdu'l-Bahá*, p. 273.

[89] Ibid., p. 204.

[90] Ibid., pp. 1-2.

[91] From a new translation provided by the Bahá'í World Center. Cf. *Tablets of Abdul-Baha*, Vol. 1, p. 37.

[92] From *The Will and Testament of 'Abdu'l-Bahá*, pp. 13-14.

[93] From a talk given by 'Abdu'l-Bahá at an interracial gathering at the home of Mr. and Mrs. Joseph H. Hannen, Washington, D.C., November 10, 1912. Notes by Joseph H. Hannen. *Promulgation*, pp. 425-28.

[94] From *Selections from the Writings of 'Abdu'l-Bahá*, p. 291-92.

[95] From a talk given by 'Abdu'l-Bahá at the Geneological Hall, New York, November 17, 1912. Notes by Edna McKinney. *Promulgation*, p. 439.

[96] From *Selections from the Writings of 'Abdu'l-Bahá*, p. 31-32.

[97] From an address given by 'Abdu'l-Bahá at Pembroke Chapel, Liverpool, England, December 15, 1912. Notes by Isabel Fraser. *Star of the West*, Vol. 3 (January 19, 1913) no. 17, pp. 4-5.

[98] From a talk given by 'Abdu'l-Bahá in Paris. October 16, 1912. In *Paris Talks*, p. 16.

[99] From *The Will and Testament of 'Abdu'l-Bahá*, p. 14.

[100] *Promulgation*, p. 348.

[101] From *Selections from the Writings of 'Abdu'l-Bahá*, p. 2.

[102] From a new translation provided by the Bahá'í World Center. Cf. *Tablets of Abdul-Baha*, Vol. 3, pp. 641-42.

'Abdu'l-Bahá

[103] From a new translation provided by the Bahá'í World Center. Cf. *Tablets of Abdul-Baha*, Vol. 2, p. 318-19.
Assembly of the Bahá'ís of the City of New York, 1987.

Bibliography

'Abdu'l-Bahá. *'Abdu'l-Bahá in London.* London: Bahá'í Publishing Trust, 1921 (1982).

————. "Addresses by 'Abdu'l-Bahá in California." Ella Cooper papers. National Bahá'í Archives, Wilmette, Ill.

————. *Memorials of the Faithful.* Wilmette, Ill.: Bahá'í Publishing Trust, 1971.

————. *Paris Talks: Addresses given by 'Abdu'l-Bahá in Paris in 1911-1912.* London: Bahá'í Publishing Trust, 1912 (1972).

————. *The Promulgation of Universal Peace: Talks Delivered by 'Abdu'l-Bahá during His Visit to the United States and Canada in 1912.* Revised Edition. Comp. by Howard MacNutt. Wilmette, Ill.: Bahá'í Publishing Trust, 1912 (1982).

————. *Selections from the Writings of 'Abdu'l-Bahá.* Haifa: Bahá'í World Centre, 1978.

————. *Some Answered Questions.* Wilmette, Ill.: Bahá'í Publishing Trust, 1908 (1981).

————. *Tablets of Abdul-Baha Abbas.* 3 vols. Chicago: Bahá'í Publishing Society, 1909-1916.

————. "Tablet to Dr. August Henri Forel," *Bahá'í World*, vol. 15 (1968-1973) pp. 37-43. Haifa: Bahá'í World Centre, 1976.

————. *Will and Testament of 'Abdu'l-Bahá.* Wilmette, Ill.: Bahá'í Publishing Trust, 1944 (1971).

'Abdu'l-Bahá in Canada. Rev. Ed. Thornhill, Ontario: Bahá'í Canada Publications, 1962 (1987).

'Abdu'l-Bahá

Ahdieh, Hussein and Hopson, Eliane A. *'Abdu'l-Bahá in New York: The City of the Covenant.* New York: The Spiritual Assembly of the Bahá''ís of New York, 1987.

Bahá'í Prayers: A Selection of Prayers Revealed by Bahá'u'lláh, the Báb, and 'Abdu'l-Bahá. Wilmette, Ill.: Bahá'í Publishing Trust, 1982.

Baha'i Scriptures: Selections from the Utterances of Baha'u'llah and Abdul-Baha. 2nd Edition. Comp. by Horace Holley. New York: Bahá'í Publishing Committee, 1928.

Bahá'í World Faith: Selected Writings of Bahá'u'lláh and 'Abdu'l-Bahá. 2nd Edition. Wilmette, Ill.: Bahá'í Publishing Trust, 1956.

Balyuzi, Hasan M. *'Abdu'l-Bahá: The Center of the Covenant of Bahá'u'lláh.* Oxford: George Ronald, 1971.

Blomfield, Lady. *The Chosen Highway.* Wilmette, Ill.: Bahá'í Publishing Trust, 1940 (1967).

Brown, Ramona Allen. *Memories of 'Abdu'l-Bahá.* Wilmette, Ill.: Bahá'í Publishing Trust, 1980.

Browne, E. G., ed., *A Traveller's Narrative.* Cambridge University Press, 1891.

Chase, Thornton. *In Galilee.* Reprint. Los Angeles: Kalimát Press, 1985.

Dodge, Wendell Phillips. "Abdul-Baha's Arrival in America," *Star of the West,* Vol. 3 (April 28, 1912) no. 3, pp. 3-6.

Esslemont, John E. *Bahá'u'lláh and the New Era.* 3rd Edition. Wilmette, Ill.: Bahá'í Publishing Trust, 1923 (1970).

Esty, Frances, comp. *The Garden of the Heart: From the Writings of Bahá'u'lláh and 'Abdu'l-Bahá.* Buffalo, New York, 1930.

Fádil, Jináb-i, "The Divine Servant—The Life of 'Abdu'l-
Bahá," *Star of the West*, vol. 15 (June 1924) no. 3, pp. 73-
78 and vol. 16 (July 1924) no. 4, pp. 108-111.

Faizi, A. Q., trans. *Stories from the Delight of Hearts: The Memoirs of
Mírzá Haydar-'Alí*. Los Angeles: Kalimát Press, 1980.

Michael Fitzgerald, ed. *The Creative Circle: Art, Literature, and
Music in Bahá'í Perspective*. Los Angeles: Kalimát Press,
1989.

Ford, Mary Hanford. "The Economic Teaching of Abdul-
Baha," *Star of the West*, Vol. 8 (March 21, 1917) no. 1, pp.
3-7, 11-16.

———. *The Oriental Rose*. New York: Broadway Publishing
Co., 1910.

Gail, Marzieh. "Florence Breed Khanum," *Bahá'í World*, Vol.
12 (1950-1954) pp. 703-4. Wilmette, Ill.: Bahá'í Publishing Trust, 1956.

———. *The Sheltering Branch*. Wilmette, Ill.: Bahá'í Publishing
Trust, 1959 (1970).

Gibran, Jean and Gibran, Kahlil. *Kahlil Gibran: His Life and World*.
Brooklyn, New York: Interlink Publishing Group, 1991.

Goodall, Helen S. and Cooper, Ella Goodall. *Daily Lessons
Received at 'Akká, January 1908*. Wilmette, Ill.: Bahá'í
Publishing Trust, 1908 (1979).

Grundy, Julia M. *Ten Days in the Light of 'Akká*. Wilmette, Ill.:
Bahá'í Publishing Trust, 1907 (1979).

Haney, Charles and Mariam. *A Heavenly Feast: Some Utterances of
Abdul-Baha to Two American Pilgrims in Acca, Syria, February
1909*. N.p., 1910.

Honnold, Annamarie, ed. *Vignettes from the Life of 'Abdu'l-Bahá.* Oxford: George Ronald, 1982.

Ives, Howard Colby. *Portals to Freedom.* London: George Ronald, 1962.

Jaxon, Honore J., "A Stroll with Abdul-Baha," *Star of the West,* Vol. 3 (May 17, 1912) no. 4, pp. 27-29.

Kazemzadeh, Kazem and Kazemzadeh, Firuz, "Five Books About 'Abdu'l-Bahá," *World Order: A Bahá'í Magazine,* vol. 6 (Fall 1971) no. 1, pp. 76-84.

Maxwell, May. *An Early Pilgrimage.* Rev. Ed. Oxford: George Ronald, 1917 (1969).

The Mystery of God. Rev. Ed. Comp. by Iran Furutan Muhajer. London: Bahá'í Publishing Trust, 1979.

Nakhjavani, Violette. *Amatu'l-Bahá Visits India.* 2nd Ed. New Delhi: Bahá'í Publishing Trust, 1966 (1984).

The Passing of 'Abdu'l-Bahá: A Compilation. Los Angeles: Kalimát Press, 1991.

Phelps, Myron H. *The Life and Teachings of Abbas Effendi* (New York: G. P. Putnam's Songs, 1903 [*The Master in 'Akká.* Los Angeles: Kalimát Press, 1985].

Rabb, Mrs. Mary M., comp., "The Divine Art of Living," *Star of the West,* vol. 7 (1916-1917) nos. 16, 18; vol. 8 (1917-1918) nos. 2, 4, 6, 8, 10, 11, 18, 19.

————., "Studies in Immortality," *Star of the West,* Vol. 14 (April 1923) no. 1, pp. 8-12; vol. 14 (May 1923) no. 2, pp. 35-42.

Thompson, Juliet. *The Diary of Juliet Thompson.* Los Angeles: Kalimát Press, 1983.

Townshend, George. *'Abdu'l-Bahá: The Master.* Oxford: George Ronald, 1987.

——. "The Way of the Master," *The Bahá'í World: A Biennial International Record,* vol. 4 (1930-1932) pp. 337-43. Wilmette, Ill.: Bahá'í Publishing Trust, 1933.

Utterances of Abdul Beha Abbas to Two Young Men, American Pilgrims to Acre, 1901. New York: Board of Counsel, 1901.

Wilhelm, Roy; Cobb, Stanwood; and Coy, Genevieve. *In His Presence: Visits to 'Abdu'l-Bahá.* Los Angeles: Kalimát Press, 1989.

[Wilhelm, Roy and Mills, Mountford J.] *Glimpses of Abdul Baha Prior to 1908 A.D by 'Roy' and M.J.M.* N.p., 1908.

Yúnis Khán-i Afrúkhtih. *Kitáb-i Khátirát-i Nuh Sáliby-i 'Akká.* Tehran: Bahá'í Publishing Trust, 109 B.E.

BOOKS OF RELATED INTEREST

Ways in Mystery: Explorations in Mystical Awareness and Life by Luther Askeland. "Full of grace, profound insight and wisdom" *Publishers Weekly* $17 / paperback

Creation and the Timeless Order of Things: Essays in Islamic Mystical Philosophy by Toshihiko Izutsu. Seven seminal essays on mystical Islam. $16 / paperback

The Green Sea of Heaven: Fifty ghazals from the Diwan of Hafiz, translated by Elizabeth Gray. A groundbreaking work of translation of Hafiz's sublime sacred poetry. $14.95 / paperback

Common Era: Best New Writings on Religion, edited by Steven Scholl. "A striking and significant anthology" *Publishers Weekly* $14.95 / paperback

SAGA: Best New Writings on Mythology, edited by Jonathan Young. "Highly recommended" *Library Journal* $14.95 / paperback

KAHLIL GIBRAN TRANSLATION SERIES

The Beloved: Reflections on the Path of the Heart $17 / cloth
The Vision: Reflections on the Way of the Soul $17 / cloth
The Storm: Stories and Prose Poems $18 / cloth
Spirit Brides $16 / cloth

These and other titles on religion are available from:
White Cloud Press, PO Box 3400, Ashland, Oregon 97520.
Web site: http://www.jeffnet.org/whitecloud. Phone 1-800-380-8286